Lincoln
Centennial Association
Papers

Lincoln
Centennial Association
Papers

Delivered Before the Members of the
Lincoln Centennial Association

INTRODUCTION

By Logan Hay, President, Lincoln Centennial Association

❂ ❂ ❂

WHERE LINCOLN PRACTICED LAW

By Paul M. Angle, Executive Secretary, Lincoln Centennial
Association

❂ ❂ ❂

LINCOLN'S LAST STRUGGLE—VICTORY?

By William E. Dodd, Professor of History, University of
Chicago

at Springfield, Illinois, on
February 12, 1927

Springfield, Illinois
LINCOLN CENTENNIAL ASSOCIATION
1927

PRINTED BY R. R. DONNELLEY & SONS CO., THE LAKESIDE PRESS, CHICAGO

Foreword

THE present volume—the Lincoln Centennial Association Papers for 1927—is the fourth volume in the series. Like its predecessors it consists of the addresses delivered before the members of the Lincoln Centennial Association on the last anniversary of Lincoln's birth, in this case February 12, 1927.

In the foregoing volumes it has been customary to summarize in a short foreword the work of the Association during the year for which the volume is issued. Brevity limits that summary to outstanding developments only.

During the current year the Association has acquired permanent office quarters. Early in the year routine office work had reached such proportions that it absorbed practically all the time of the executive secretary. Stenographic help became a necessity, yet it was impossible in the quarters the Association occupied in the Sangamo Club. Therefore an arrangement was made with the Illinois State Bar Association by which the Lincoln Centennial Association was to share its offices in the First National Bank Building and to have the services of its office staff. The arrangement is working very satisfactorily.

Because of the relief thus afforded its secretary the Association was able to undertake a more ambitious program of research and publication. That program called for the publication of two day-by-day records of Lincoln's life during 1927, the issuance of bulletins every three months, and the speedy completion of the secretary's investigation of Lincoln's career as a circuit lawyer. In accordance with the program, "Lincoln in the Year 1859" was issued in August. "Lincoln in the Year 1860" is complete and ready for the press. Two quarterly bulletins have been issued, and the third will be mailed to members on December 1, the date of its scheduled appearance. By February 12, 1928, the secretary's work on Lincoln's career in the trial courts will have been finished, and will form the subject of his address on that date.

In addition to the prompt realization of this program, the Association has made progress along two other lines of historical endeavor. Its collection of Lincoln photostats, particularly photostats of Lincoln legal papers, has increased materially. And much has been done in gathering together unpublished and uncollected Lincoln letters and speeches. It will not be long before the Association will be able to issue a full sized volume of these letters and speeches. Such a volume will be an outstanding contribution to Lincolniana.

The membership of the Association has increased slowly but steadily, until at the present time it numbers well over six hundred. The endowment fund is growing, although not so rapidly as the officers hoped. A list of members and contributors to endowment will be found at the end of this volume.

Springfield, Illinois,
November 1, 1927.

Introduction

BY LOGAN HAY

President, Lincoln Centennial Association

Introduction

FELLOW Citizens and Members of the Lincoln Centennial Association:

About a year ago the America-Japan Society, at the instance of Col. Burnett, Military Attache of the Legation of the United States, a brother of our townsman, Samuel T. Burnett, brought about the writing of a large number of essays upon Lincoln by Japanese students in the schools of Japan corresponding to our high schools and junior colleges. These papers were written in competition for Lincoln medals offered as prizes by one of our local institutions. About sixty of the best papers were sent to the Executive Secretary of the Lincoln Centennial Association to be judged, and on the basis of his judgment, the prizes were awarded.

I read perhaps a dozen of these papers. I was not surprised to find references to Lincoln's election as President, to his official acts and to the manner of his death. I was surprised to find the very considerable part of these papers which told of the incidents of his life before he became President; of his birth and boyhood in Kentucky, of his youth in Indiana, of his young manhood in New Salem and of the quarter century of his life as a citizen of Springfield. They disclosed a surprising knowledge of incidents, of personal associates, and of places connected with Lincoln's activities, before he became President.

The growing generation of students in other foreign lands and in this country have a like interest in, and knowledge of, Lincoln's life before he became President. Many of these students will come to Springfield and New Salem to see the places connected with Lincoln's life. If they find that our Lincoln lore is a living thing to us, their pilgrimage will not have been in vain. If they find that our Lincoln traditions, known to them, have been forgotten by us, they will be grievously disappointed.

Let me illustrate by a personal experience. As a boy I read and re-read with the deepest interest "Tom Brown's School Days." The incidents and places connected with the author's life at Rugby were alive to me. When I went to England I visited Rugby. I asked to see the spot where Tom Brown had fought Slogger Williams. But the name Tom Brown did not register with my guide or suggest to him any associations.

"Tom Brown's School Days" have never been so real to me since that visit of disappointment. Had my

guide taken me to the spot of the fight and recalled its incidents, and then to the bench in the school where Tom had carved his initials and to the scenes of the other incidents of which Hughes tells, my visit to Rugby would have been a thing of joy, pleasant to recall.

The custom of having, at each of our annual meetings, held on the recurring anniversaries of Lincoln's birth, a paper on one of the places connected with some phase of Lincoln's life as a resident of Springfield, continually keeps the community familiar with our Lincoln traditions. The publication of the proceedings of these annual meetings preserves these traditions for the future and makes them available for the Lincoln student, wherever he may be. From year to year we are recalling to this community and making available to others chapter after chapter of the story of Lincoln's Springfield.

These annual meetings in this hall will ever keep this community mindful of the many associations of this room and building with the public life of Lincoln, a story which was so well told by Henry A. Converse at our meeting three years ago. Two years ago A. L. Bowen told us of the Lincoln Home.

A year ago Paul M. Angle gave us the story of the monument at Oak Ridge. Today he is to speak to us

on a more lively subject, "Where Lincoln Practiced Law."

Mr. Angle is, as you know, Executive Secretary of the Lincoln Centennial Association. He devotes his full time to the work of the Association. He has been with us now a year and a half, and I cannot speak too highly of the accurate and thorough work which Mr. Angle is doing. He is continually unearthing— I use the term accurately—from the dust-buried records hitherto unknown information in regard to the Illinois period of Lincoln's life. Yesterday it was some forgotten and supposedly lost election registers, showing the candidates for whom Lincoln voted in the days when voters delivered their votes by word of mouth and not by ballot. Today it is a law office, occupied by Lincoln early in his practice, unmarked, long since forgotten, and, I believe, unmentioned by any of Lincoln's biographers: Mr. Angle.

Where Lincoln Practiced Law

Delivered by MR. PAUL M. ANGLE *before the Lincoln Centennial Association, in the Circuit Court Room, Springfield, Illinois, February 12, 1927.*

Where Lincoln Practiced Law

W HEN, on April 15, 1837, Abraham Lincoln entered Springfield with the intent of residing there permanently, he came to what would now be called a "boom town." Slow and somnolent a few months before, its life had been quickened with a sharp start when, on February 28, the legislature had passed the act locating there the seat of the state government. An impromptu celebration had taken place when the little town of ten or twelve hundred people heard the news. The "groceries" had a record day—a day which culminated in the destruction of the public square's most gruesome ornament, the whipping post, which, when surrounded with crates and boxes and saturated with tar, disappeared in a blazing fire.

Nor did this enthusiasm burn itself out in one day of riotous rejoicing. No doubt there were aching heads and depressed spirits the morning after, but these soon gave way to a pervasive optimism generated by the hope of material rewards to follow. The editor of the *Sangamo Journal* expressed the popular attitude when he declared that the selection of Spring-field as the state capital had given new life and spirits to its citizens. "The owner of real estate sees his property rapidly enhancing in value; the merchant anticipates a large accession to our population, and a correspondent additional sale for his goods; the mechanic already has more contracts offered him for building and improvement than he can execute; the farmer anticipates, in the growth of a large and important town, a market for the varied products of his farm; indeed, every class of our citizens look to the future with confidence that we trust, will not be disappointed." Surely Lincoln could not have chosen a better time for his removal.

Riding into town on that April day, and dismounting before the store of A. Y. Ellis & Co., of which his friend Joshua Speed was part owner,[1] the young lawyer was in surroundings by no means unfamiliar. In the center of the square stood the Court House, soon to be removed to make room for the State Capitol Building. For years Lincoln had been a familiar figure in this primitive house of government. More than once he had trudged in from New Salem with the poll book of an election which he had clerked. Often, when the County Commissioners Court was in session, he had appeared in person to present the report of a road

[1]Record Book C, p. 381.   In office of Sangamon County Circuit Clerk.

survey, and to collect moneys due him for services of that and other kinds. But most important of all, it was in this building that he commenced his career as a practicing attorney.

There has been much controversy over the exact date of Lincoln's admission to the bar of Illinois. The statute in force at the time provided that before an applicant could be admitted to practice as an attorney and counsellor at law, he must not only have obtained a license, but must also have presented himself to the Clerk of the Supreme Court for enrollment. Lincoln's license was issued September 9, 1836, and for many years that was accepted as the date of his admission to the bar. Then it was discovered that his enrollment did not take place until March 1, 1837. Since, according to the statute, enrollment was as necessary as the issuance of a license, in recent years March 1, 1837, has been accepted as the date from which Lincoln's career as a lawyer is to be reckoned.

But regardless of the statute, Lincoln tried his first case in the Sangamon Circuit Court during the October term, 1836.[1] Court was held in the old brick Court House, Stephen T. Logan was on the bench, and Stephen A. Douglas was present as state's attorney. Lincoln, together with Stuart and Dummer, defended one David Wolldridge in three different actions—as-

[1] For the documents in this case see Weik, *The Real Lincoln*, pp. 134-138.

sumpsit, trespass and replevin—brought by James P. Hawthorne. After four consecutive days of stiff legal skirmishing the cases were continued until the March term, 1837, and then compromised in such a manner that neither side seems to have been victorious. Walker and Hewitt, Springfield attorneys, acted for Hawthorne, while among other members of the bar one finds such familiar names as Dan Stone, George Forquer, S. H. Treat, and E. D. Baker.

What do we know about this primitive building where Abraham Lincoln commenced his legal career? Built in 1831, the brick court house was the third to be constructed in Sangamon County, but the first to be placed in the public square. It was a square structure two stories high, topped by a hip roof, and ornamented with a cupola from which spectators were in the habit of viewing the town below. John Moffett and David S. Taylor drew the plans, and were rewarded for that service by an order on the county treasurer for $3.00, later supplemented by a second order for $2.00. Work on the building was commenced in the spring of 1831, but such finishing touches as glazing and plastering were not completed until late in the following year.

When finished, the new court house was far more than a place where courts were held and routine governmental business carried on. Its location in the square, for instance, was the occasion for the entire business district to shift from its original center at Second and Jefferson Streets to the public square, where it has remained ever since. The county authorities were quick to take advantage of this change, and to let out the second floor of the building for commercial purposes. There Simeon Francis printed the *Sangamo Journal,* and there Dan Stone wrote briefs and drew mortgages and deeds. In time, however, this came to be an unsatisfactory arrangement, and late in 1835 the county commissioners ordered the building cleared of all its occupants. But it still continued to be the center of the community, for the sheriff was directed to employ some suitable person whose duty it should be to have "the well attended to and to accommodate those who may desire to go into the Court House having business proper to be done there during the intervals of Court or to view the House or the Country from the top thereof or for the purpose of worshiping on the Sabbath."

A structure of so much importance in the community was naturally one of the "points of interest" to which all newcomers were speedily introduced. One such has left us a vivid picture of the scene which greeted him when, in the autumn of 1835, he was conducted to the court house by his guide. "The court was in session, and a case was then in progress. Judge

Logan was on the bench, and Mr. Douglas (the 'Little Giant,' as he was afterwards called) on the floor. To us, just from the city of New York, with the sleek lawyers and the prim and dignified judges, and audiences to correspond, there was a contrast so great, that it was almost impossible to repress a burst of laughter. Upon the bench was seated the judge, with his chair tilted back and his heels as high as his head, and in his mouth a veritable corn cob pipe; his hair standing nine ways for Sunday, while his clothing was more like that worn by a woodchopper than anybody else. There was a railing that divided the audience; outside of which smoking and chewing and spitting of tobacco seemed to be the principal employment."[1]

In some such surroundings Abraham Lincoln tried his first case. That, however, was while he was still a resident of New Salem. When he arrived in Springfield on April 15, 1837, what was Springfield like? Suppose he had decided to have one last look from the cupola of the court house so soon to be removed— what would he have seen below him?

At that time of the year the streets surrounding the square were probably a wallow of mud almost impassable. Lining those streets were the town's business houses, in the main one story frame buildings, dotted here and there with two story brick structures, but

[1]R. H. Beach in *History of Sangamon County*, (1881), p. 183.

just as frequently with log cabins, still very much in use. These buildings housed in all "nineteen dry-goods stores, one wholesale and six retail groceries, four drug stores, one book-store and two clothing stores," while in them and adjacent buildings "eleven lawyers and eighteen physicians, including steam doctors," had their offices. In the middle of Sixth Street, just north of Washington, stood the market house, a brick building in which the farmers of the vicinity could display and sell their produce direct to the purchaser. West of the market house was Johnson's Row, one section of the series of ramshackle one story frame buildings which faced the north side of the square, and which, because of their dilapidated appearance, were usually designated "Chicken Row." On the north side of Jefferson Street, between Sixth and Seventh, was the county jail, also a brick structure and probably one of some distinction, since it has been designed by the same man who drew the plans for the old State House. In addition to the court house, the market house and the jail, there were several quasi-public buildings, the churches. Of these, in the spring of 1837, there were "houses of worship for two Presbyterian churches, one Baptist Reformer, one Methodist, one Episcopalian, and one Baptist society, all of which have ministers and respectable congregations."[1]

[1]This paragraph is based in the main upon the anonymous gazeteer, *"Illinois in 1837,"* p. 129.

Early in 1837 the observer would have noticed, conspicuous among the surrounding frame buildings, a row of several new, two story brick buildings commencing at the northwest corner of Fifth and Washington Streets and extending northward. Inquiring for the drug store of A. W. Hughes, he would have been directed not to such and such a number, North Fifth Street, but to Number Four Hoffman's Row, for such was the name of this row of stores, and in 1837, street names were not used by Springfieldians in daily intercourse. It was in this row of buildings, but at Number Four, *upstairs,* that Abraham Lincoln commenced the practice of the law with John T. Stuart.

Hoffman's Row consisted of six stores,[1] each forty-four feet deep, and, roughly speaking, twenty feet wide. As to appearances, we know little more than that they were two stories in height and built of brick. By reason of both these facts, however, they were the outstanding business buildings in the Springfield of 1837, where most of the structures were one story high and built of wood. Exactly when this row of stores was built we cannot say. However, construction could not have been commenced prior to November 17, 1835, when Hoffman obtained the property on the corner of Fifth and Washington Streets, and it is

[1]Statement of Dr. William Jayne, Feb. 4, 1908. In possession of E. D. Keys.

probable that nothing was done before May 1, 1836, when he obtained possession of the west half of the corner lot. Building operations would have been very difficult, on account of the weather, much before that time. Then too, newspaper advertisements contain no references to Hoffman's Row before the last few weeks of 1836. It is probable that construction was commenced about May, 1836, and completed in the late autumn of the same year.

Hoffman's Row was considered "a striking and handsome improvement upon the other buildings" of the city. Stuart and Lincoln might well have been proud when they took up their quarters there—No. 4 Hoffman's Row, upstairs, meant new surroundings for Stuart as well as Lincoln; for the office of Stuart and Dummer, the preceding partnership, had been located elsewhere—for certainly no other lawyers of the town had a better office, and probably few had one nearly so good.

Hoffman's Row took its name from Herman L. Hoffman, who, while not the sole owner, possessed by far the largest interest in the property. It is curious that a name for many years in common usage in Springfield should have been derived from one who never lived there. A native New Yorker, Hoffman, "with his doctor's degree in his pocket and his worldly goods in a valise," had removed to St. Louis in the fall of 1819. There, to supplement his professional earnings, he opened a drug store. He was successful, and at the end of four or five years was regarded as a prosperous man. Whether his marriage to a daughter of Major Joseph Klein, reputedly Springfield's wealthiest citizen, was the cause of his interest in Springfield real estate, or whether that interest led to the marriage, is a matter for speculation, but at any rate, during the thirties, Hoffman was the owner of considerable property in Springfield and the adjacent country. Incidentally, during a trip to Illinois in 1835 —very likely at the time he was acquiring the land for the "Row"—the stage in which he was riding tipped over, and his right hand was so badly injured that amputation was necessary. Although he spent some years in Cincinnati and Cleveland, Hoffman was well known as one of the most prominent citizens of St. Louis, where he died at an advanced age.

On the 15th of April, 1837, came the announcement of a new Springfield law firm: "J. T. Stuart and A. Lincoln, Attorneys and Counsellors at Law, will practice, conjointly, in the Courts of this Judicial Circuit.—Office No. 4 Hoffman's Row, upstairs."[1] The same issue of the *Sangamo Journal* announced also that A. W. Hughes, "Dealer in Drugs, Medicines, Paints, Dye-stuffs, Window glass, etc., has removed

[1]*Sangamo Journal,* April 15, 1837. Notice dated April 12.

to No. 4, Hoffman's Row—where he will be most happy to wait on the public." Yet Herndon states as a fact—which is well supported by local tradition—that the Stuart and Lincoln office was above the room temporarily used as the county court room. This room was No. 5 Hoffman's Row. The inescapable conclusion is that Lincoln's office was actually located above No. 5, but that entrance to it could be had only through the store room next door. That Stuart and Lincoln were not located above the drug store is proved by a notice which appeared in the *Sangamo Journal* for June 17, 1837, in which Dr. A. G. Henry announced the removal of his office to Hoffman's Row, upstairs, immediately over Hughes' Drug Store.

Stuart and Lincoln remained together for four full years. During all that time they kept their office in Hoffman's Row—an evidence of stability exceptional in a day when merchants and professional men changed their places of business every few months. Of the interior we have but one picture. "The furniture was in keeping with the pretentions of the firm—a small lounge or bed, a chair containing a buffalo robe, in which the junior member was wont to sit and study, a hard wooden bench, a feeble attempt at a bookcase, and a table which answered for a desk."[1]

[1]Herndon, *Life of Lincoln*, (1889 ed.) I., 184.

In May, 1841, Lincoln severed his connection with Stuart, and became the junior partner of Stephen T. Logan. In Springfield it has always been thought that the office of this firm was located in the building which still stands on the southeast corner of the public square, and the building has been marked with a bronze tablet. But the newspaper notice gives the Logan and Lincoln office location as "opposite Hoffman's Row,"[1] thus placing it on the east side of North Fifth Street within a hundred and twenty feet from the corner of Fifth and Washington. Consequently the city of Springfield possesses another historic site, the very existence of which has long been forgotten.

At this late date it is impossible to do much more than guess at the exact location of this office, and at the character of the structure in which it was situated. It is probable, however, that the office was in a building on the same site as that now owned by Mr. John W. Black, 108-110 North Fifth Street.[2] That there

[1] *Sangamo Journal,* May 14, 1841.

[2] Two well informed old residents of Springfield have some recollection of this Logan and Lincoln location. Mr. George H. Helmle says that Dr. William Jayne told him that Logan & Lincoln once occupied an office in the Black building, still standing at 108-110 N. Fifth St. Mr. A. G. Murray says that some years after Lincoln's death his brother, Mr. G. W. Murray, and W. H. Herndon had a law office in the Black building. He visited them there often, and remembers that "Uncle Billy Herndon" was accustomed to relate that years before he (Herndon) and Lincoln occupied that very room. This I think to be a mistake. In all probability Herndon simply said that years before, Lincoln occupied a room in the same building, or in an earlier building on the same spot. A painting

was a structure of some kind on this site as early as 1841 is proved by the newspaper notice of Dr. E. H. Merryman, which gives his office location as opposite Wallace and Diller. (Wallace and Diller were drug merchants who in 1841 occupied the Hughes' store at No. 4 Hoffman's Row.) As to the character of the building, it was probably frame and one story in height.

The Logan and Lincoln partnership lasted from the spring of 1841 until the autumn of 1844—three and a half years instead of two as generally thought.[1]

---

of the north side of the square, made in the 50's and now hanging in the lobby of the St. Nicholas Hotel, shows very clearly that the Black building, a three-story brick, had not yet been erected.

[1]William H. Herndon, (*Life,* II, 265-6) sets 1843 as the date of the termination of Lincoln's partnership with Logan and the formation of the firm of Lincoln and Herndon. Later biographers have become more specific, naming September 20, 1843, as the date on which the firm of Logan and Lincoln was dissolved and the firm of Lincoln and Herndon formed. (See Weik, *The Real Lincoln,* p. 139; Newton, *Lincoln and Herndon,* p. 19.) I have never seen this statement supported by the citation of any authority whatever.

On the other hand, there is ample proof that the firm of Logan and Lincoln endured at least a year later than September, 1843. Their card continued to appear in the *Sangamo Journal* until March 27, 1845, when, unaccompanied by any notice of dissolution or of the formation of a succeeding firm, it is printed for the last time. But lawyers were so careless about changing their newspaper cards that this date can hardly be taken as the terminal one. That Logan and Lincoln were in actual association in 1844 is proved by the following documents: Declaration in Dresser vs. Guest, drawn by Lincoln and signed Logan & Lincoln, p. q; filed March 20, 1844. (Original in Library of Brown University.) Petition for divorce in Wilson vs. Wilson, drawn by Lincoln and signed Logan & Lincoln, Sols. for complaint; filed May 3, 1844. (Photostat in Lincoln Centennial Association collection.) Moreover, we have Lincoln's

But unlike the preceding partnership, this firm occupied offices in two different locations. Just how long they remained on North Fifth Street we do not know —the most that can be said is that late in February, 1843, they were still situated "opposite Hoffman's Row." On the other hand, we know that by August, 1844, they had moved to the building which stands on the southwest corner of Sixth and Adams Streets and which is generally designated the "old Farmers Bank Building."[1] At that time this building housed the post

own statement as to the duration of the partnership. In a letter dated September 13, 1853, to George B. Kinkead of Lexington, Kentucky, Lincoln writes: "I can prove . . . by Stephen T. Logan of Springfield, Illinois, that he & I were partners from the Spring of 1841 to the autumn of 1844."

It is difficult to fix the exact date when the Logan and Lincoln partnership was dissolved and the Lincoln-Herndon partnership formed. The Bar Docket of the Illinois Supreme Court, 1842-1846, (in office of Clerk of the Supreme Court, Springfield, Illinois) shows that one *new* case—Blankenship vs. Center—was docketed for Logan and Lincoln at the December term, 1844. And, while Logan and Lincoln appear individually or in association with other attorneys—as they had done since the beginning of their partnership—they are never on opposing sides of the same case during this term. Moreover, Herndon was not admitted to the bar until December 9, 1844 (Roll of Attorneys, Office of Clerk of Supreme Court, Springfield, Illinois.)

While the foregoing court records point to some date in the early winter, rather than in the autumn, of 1844 as the terminal date, they do not prove Lincoln's statement erroneous. Herndon might well have become Lincoln's partner a few weeks before his admission to the bar. And the new Supreme Court case at the December term, may very well have been one which Logan and Lincoln had accepted prior to the dissolution of the firm. In the absence of other evidence Lincoln's own statement, that he and Logan were partners until "the autumn of 1844," must stand in lieu of an exact date.

[1]*Sangamo Journal*, Feb. 23, 1843, and same for Aug. 22, 1844. No copies of the paper are available for the period between these dates.

office, and the Logan and Lincoln card read, "Office over the Post office—third story."

This building, no less than the Hoffman's Row block, was for its time one of the town's show places. Its construction was commenced in 1840, and January of the following year saw it ready for occupancy. Not only was it the first three story building to be erected on the south side of the square, but it was also said to be the finest business house in central Illinois. S. M. Tinsley, a Springfield merchant, was the owner, and the actual work of construction was done under the supervision of a Pennsylvanian named Martin.

An art exhibit marked the opening of the new structure. On January 27, 1841, an "Exhibition of Paintings" consisting of "Upwards of one hundred highly finished drawings, in water colours, miniatures, etc.," was advertised as being on display in "S. M. Tinsley's new building." A month later notice was given that S. M. Tinsley & Co. "Have removed their entire stock of Goods to the New 4 story [four by counting a sort of half floor at the top] brick building, on the southeast corner of the public square . . . where they have on hand a good stock of staple and Fancy Goods which will be sold cheap to cash or short time punctual customers, and to our old and tried friends on the usual terms." Very soon the United States Government rented a part of the building for the use of the United States Circuit and District Courts, and for several years the post office was located there also.

We are fortunate in having a description of the interior of the office Lincoln and Herndon occupied in the Tinsley Building. "The furniture," says one who was once a student there,[1] "somewhat dilapidated, consisted of one small desk and a table, a sofa or lounge with a raised head at one end, and a half-dozen plain wooden chairs. The floor was never scrubbed. If cleaned at all it was done by the clerk or law student who occasionally ventured to sweep up the accumulated dirt. Over the desk a few shelves had been enclosed; this was the office bookcase holding a set of Blackstone, Kent's Commentaries, Chitty's Pleadings, and a few other books."

In a short time, however, Herndon took a hand in the interest of more and better office equipment. A year after the formation of the partnership he purchased a desk for $20.00 and books to the amount of $54.65. In June, 1846, he bought more books, another desk, and a table, $13.00 covering the cost of both articles of furniture. Several miscellaneous expenses in September and October brought his total expenditures up to $98.64, of which Lincoln's share was one half, $49.32.

[1]Gibson W. Harris as quoted in Weik, *The Real Lincoln,* p. 106. Harris writes of the office as he knew it in 1845.

But Lincoln had already met a part of his share of this expense. On January 1, 1846, Herndon had credited him with $35.00—$25.00 in cash and the balance in the form of a note signed Grant and Herndon. Other small credits were made at later dates —usually cash from individuals, presumably Lincoln's clients—so that at the time of the accounting Lincoln's indebtedness had dwindled to a small amount.[1]

Most students agree that it was his association with Logan that made Abraham Lincoln a real lawyer. A raw novice when Stuart took him in in 1837, he left Logan seven and a half years later an attorney with an established reputation. As Lincoln had grown in his profession, so had the city of his adoption. In 1844 Abraham Lincoln could have looked back over his few years of residence and noted many changes— many changes in the city generally, and many changes in the conditions of his own work.

The little brick court house in which Lincoln had tried his first case had been torn down soon after his arrival in Springfield, and in its place in the center of the square now stood the State House, which, while not yet completely finished, had been in use for several years. Sangamon County and Springfield had contributed heavily toward the construction of this

[1]This and the preceding paragraph are based upon Herndon's statement to Lincoln, in possession of Miss Alice Orendorff and Mrs. Edna Orendorff Macpherson, Springfield, Illinois.

building, and as a result the authorities had felt it inadvisable to erect a new court house. To supply the deficiency they rented rooms here and there for county purposes. From 1837 until 1840 court was held in Hoffman's Row, in a building on the west side of the street five doors north of Washington Street. The owner was Ninian W. Edwards, Lincoln's brother-in-law. Then for a time court was held in different places,[1] for one term in the Campbellite church,[2] for another in the Methodist Episcopal church.[3] But not for long, for the Edwards storeroom was soon rented again, and remained in use until April, 1846.

This court room—the Hoffman's Row Court House as it is often called—was directly underneath Stuart and Lincoln's office, into which entrance could be had by means of a trap door in the ceiling. One evening before Lincoln had yet become a full-fledged Springfield resident, his friend E. D. Baker was making a political speech to a crowd gathered in the court

[1]N. W. Matheny is authorized to procure "a room for holding the Circuit Court for one year commencing after the 25th July next and that he give N. W. Edwards written notice that on the 25th July next the county will deliver up to him the room now occupied by them as a court Room." County Commissioners Record, E., p. 18. Order dated June 11, 1840. In County Clerk's Office.

[2]"Ordered that Daniel B. Hill be allowed the sum of $50 for the use of the Campbellite Church as a court room." Order dated June 8, 1841. Ibid., p. 67.

[3]"Ordered that the trustees of the M. E. Church be allowed $50 for the use of church for court room." Order dated December 7, 1841. Ibid., p. 90.

room. Growing reckless, he made a charge of corruption against the democratic party in such a way that a fight seemed probable. When the situation was most tense, a long pair of legs dangled from above, and Lincoln by degrees came into view. Picking up a stone water pitcher, and threatening to break it over the head of the first person to touch Baker, he soon restored order. As was his custom, he had been lying on the floor taking in the scene below, and thus had been able to appear at just the right moment.

Lincoln's first cases were tried before justices of the peace and in the Sangamon Circuit Court, but before long new fields were opened. As soon as the state offices were transferred from Vandalia to Springfield in 1839, it was possible for the young lawyer to practice in the state Supreme Court. Until the State House was ready for occupancy the court sat in the Episcopal Church, then located on the south side of Adams Street between Third and Fourth. Late in 1840, or early in 1841, the Supreme Court moved into its quarters in the State House, occupying the northeast corner of the first (now the second) floor. Here Lincoln tried 175 law suits, many of them of great importance. Add to that the fact that here was located the State Law Library, where he spent hour after hour almost without number, and it will be realized that no building in Springfield, with the exception of the Lincoln home, surpasses the old State House in the richness of its Lincoln memories.

The State Law Library adjoined the Supreme Court chamber on the south. There the lawyers came to study their cases and prepare their briefs, and there, often as not, Lincoln could be found. Late in the day application was apt to diminish, and frequently the evenings would be given over to conviviality, and, as Herndon put it, "breezy conversation." The story tellers held forth, encouraged by the jug of whiskey which passed from hand to hand. Invariably Lincoln was the favorite, in spite of his abstinence. The lawyers would close their books, and one by one the justices of the Supreme Court would slip in from their consultations in the next room. Rarely, if Lincoln was in good trim, did these gatherings break up before midnight.

The United States Circuit and District Courts were not slow to follow the seat of the state government from Vandalia to Springfield, making the transfer in 1839. On December 3rd of that year Lincoln was admitted to practice before them. At that time Springfield possessed no Federal Building, so, as was the case with Sangamon County, it was necessary to rent rooms for the courts and their officers. Court was first held in one of the churches, but soon after the Tinsley Building was completed the court room was

located there on the second floor. For fifteen years
Lincoln tried cases in that place. Colorful years they
were, too. After 1839, and prior to 1855, the jurisdic-
tion of the United States Courts at Springfield
covered the entire state, so twice a year this building became the gathering place of Illinois' best legal
talent.

In 1855 Illinois was divided into two judicial dis-
tricts, and the United States Court in Springfield
sought new quarters. Seven rooms, providing accom-
modations for the judges, juries, clerk, marshal, district attorney and court room, were rented from
Stephen T. Logan at an annual charge of $800.[1] They
were located in a three story building, situated at the
northeast corner of Sixth and Washington Streets,
and known then as "Logan's Building." In these surroundings Lincoln tried nearly a hundred law suits.[2]
The court room was on the second floor. It was not
large, and when many spectators came—as frequently they did—not a few had to stand. The only dis-
tinctive feature of the room was the big "Cannon-
ball" stove which stood in its center, and which, in
cold weather, was fired until it became red hot. The
United States Court remained in these rooms until

[1]Letter of John Marshall, Assistant Attorney General, to author.
January 21, 1927.

[2]List compiled by author from files of U. S. District Court at Springfield, Illinois.

1870, when the present Federal Building was occupied.

During the seven and a half years of Lincoln's partnerships with Stuart and Logan, Springfield had grown. Containing between 1,000 and 1,200 people in 1837, it could now boast, and probably without much exaggeration, of 3,000. Where, in 1837, the buildings of the town were little more than a jumble of frame shacks, now there were at least some good ones. The State House was an architectural gem, although an unappreciated one. There was the State Bank building, built of the same warm brown stone, and beautiful in its simple Grecian lines. Brick business buildings, two and three stories in height, were no longer noticeable because of the rarity. And not only were the people building comfortable, attractive dwellings —they were taking pride in their surroundings. In 1845, to a disparaging critic, a local apologist was able to answer,[1] "We have few splendid gardens, but there is scarcely a lot occupied by the owner in this city that has not its garden, its shrubbery and its trees, both for fruit and ornament. The improvement exhibited here in these respects, within the last few years, has been both pleasing and striking." Even the mud of the

---

[1] *Sangamo Journal,* April 24, 1845. In the April, 1845, number of the *Albany Cultivator* a western traveller had printed some not very favorable comments on Springfield. These are reprinted in this issue of the Sangamo Journal, together with the editor's refutation.

streets, which was to remain a state-wide jest for thirty years longer, was partly atoned for by the construction of sidewalks, then being carried on enthusiastically.

It is not surprising that such a community should no longer be content to have its court room and county officers housed in rented store rooms. The financial strain caused by the erection of the State House was almost ended, and the county authorities decided that the time for action had come.

On April 5, 1845, the three county commissioners, Zachariah Peter, John Dawson and Abram Foutch, purchased from James Dunlop and Robert Irwin the lot on the southeast corner of Sixth and Washington Streets, and a month later purchased an adjoining strip from Erastus Wright. The total cost was $3,000. It is interesting to recognize, in Zachariah Peter, one of the two men who, nearly twenty-five years before, had pounded a stake in the ground near John Kelly's cabin and named the surrounding land Springfield.

The commissioners let the contract for the construction of the court house to Henry Dresser, and work was commenced at once, to be completed about a year later. The building stood on the corner of Sixth and Washington Streets, facing Sixth Street.[1] Immedi-

---

[1] For this and the following paragraph I have relied to a certain extent on pictures, but more especially on conversations with Mr. DeWitt W. Smith, Mr. George H. Helmle, Mr. James N. Garland, and Mr. George M. Brinkerhoff, all of Springfield. These men knew this building well.

ately south was the State Bank building, to which externally it bore a strong resemblance. Like the bank, it was two stories high and rectangular in shape. Six tall pillars, with their bases on a raised platform, supported a long hip roof. It was in materials that the court house gave way its inferiority to the bank building, for it was constructed of brick rather than stone, and its pillars were nothing more than sand-covered hollow wood. Through economy of this sort it had been possible to make $10,000 cover the cost of construction.

The first floor of the interior was taken up with rooms for the county officers. A wide hall way extended from the front entrance straight through to the rear, and onto this the offices opened. The court room was on the second floor. It was large—covering the entire floor except for two or three small rooms at the rear—and devoid of distinction.

In the circuit courts held in this building no attorneys were more prominent than the newly formed firm of Lincoln and Herndon. These two men continued in active practice from 1844 until 1860, and during that time Lincoln at least gained a highly respected position at the bar of Illinois. Sometime after the summer of 1849—just when we do not know —the office of the firm was transferred from the Tinsley Building on the corner of Sixth and Adams Streets to a plain unpretentious three-story brick building on the west side of the square where the Myers Building now stands.

The office was located on the second floor, "in a back room, dimly lighted by windows, apparently innocent of water and the scrub-man since creation's dawn, or the settlement of Springfield.[1]

"But the lack of translucent qualities in the windows, was compensated somewhat by the transparency of the upper half of the door leading into the hall—for there was nothing there to obstruct the perfect vision—not even a gossamer's wing, for it was perfectly diaphanous; in other words, both of the upper panels and the center piece were gone: and an agile man could readily have vaulted through the opening.

"I think there was no carpet on the floor; if so, it must have been, if in harmony with its surroundings, a marvellous fabric. And the sum total of the furnishing of the office, as I recollect it, was a rocking-chair (a favorite seat of Lincoln) and several other ordinary chairs, an old table numerously indented with a jack-knife, a wood stove, and some common bookcases, occupied for the most part with session laws and public documents. It did not seem as if the inspiration of genius could haunt such a place, and yet, in

[1]Whitney, *Life on the Circuit with Lincoln*, 458-459.

this uncouth office, the later creed of the Republican party was formulated."

It was a winter day in February, 1861. Abraham Lincoln was President-Elect of the United States. In less than twenty-four hours he would start on the long journey which was to end in Washington with his inauguration. Months ago he had turned over his law practice to his partner and devoted himself to the thousands of friends, office-hunters and merely curious who had crowded his little office in the State House. But some interest in legal matters still remained, and this afternoon he had come back to the old office to examine some papers and plan the procedure in a few cases which still held his attention. He went over the books with Herndon, and made arrangements for the completion of their unfinished business.

This done, Lincoln stretched out on the wobbly sofa. In a good humor, he spent an hour or more in reminiscing—in recalling humorous incidents of his early practice, and in laughing over many a law suit of circuit days. He started to go, hesitated, and then asked that the sign, "Lincoln & Herndon," be allowed to remain. "Give our clients to understand," he told his partner, "that the election of a President makes no change in the firm of Lincoln and Herndon." He paused for a moment, took a last look at the familiar room, and then stepped into the narrow hallway. Herndon accompanied him down the stairs. Then, after a few minutes conversation, "he disappeared down the street, and never came back to the office again."

Mr. Hay Introducing Professor Dodd

Fellow Citizens:

"Where Lincoln Practiced Law" without Lincoln would be "Hamlet" without Hamlet. And so with all our annual stories of the local Lincoln traditions. The subjects in themselves would have little interest for the world except as they touch Lincoln. In a sense, we may term these papers subjective. Lincoln is always our point of departure.

At each of these annual meetings we have a paper concerning some broader phase of Lincoln and written from an objective view point.

At our meeting three years ago Mr. McLaughlin spoke of "Lincoln as a World Figure." His point of departure was not that of a biographer of Lincoln, but that of an historian interested in and acquainted with the historical forces potent today and during the past century. He found the world today deeply interested in Lincoln, and from the view point of an historian, he tells us why. His paper is of general interest wholly aside from the personal equation of Lincoln.

And so in Dr. Finley's address at our annual meeting two years ago on "The Education of Abraham Lincoln." The approach to the subject was from the standpoint of one interested primarily in education rather than of a biographer of Lincoln. And likewise with Dr. Pupin's paper of a year since.

Today the title of our objective paper is "Lincoln's Last Struggle—Victory?" The situation and difficulties of the President of the United States during the Civil War has an interest of its own, of itself, wholly apart from personal equation of the person who occupied the office. The subject will be dealt with, not by one who has studied the Civil War period from the view point of a Lincoln biographer, but by one who for years has thoroughly studied the Civil War period and its forces and who, by reason of that study, has learned much of Lincoln and his trials during the war.

Professor Dodd was born in North Carolina shortly after the end of the Civil War. Graduating from Virginia Polytechnic Institute he pursued his historical studies in the University of Leipsic, from which he received his doctor's degree. He has taught history at Virginia Polytechnic Institute, at Randolph-Macon College and for a considerable number of years has been a member of the Department of American History at the University of Chicago. As student, teacher and writer, he is one of our foremost historians. He has taken his part in making history. He was one of the official historical advisers to Woodrow Wilson and the American representatives at the Peace Conference at Paris at the end of the World War. In that capacity he made available his knowledge of the past in aid of the solution of the problems of the present.

He has recently published an excellent 'Life of Woodrow Wilson' and is now engaged with Ray Stanard Baker in editing "The Public Papers of Woodrow Wilson." He is a frequent contributor to the leading current magazines and reviews.

From the beginning of his academic career, Professor Dodd has been interested in the southern side of the War of Secession and in the men who led that lost cause. He has written a series of biographical and historical studies which have done much to bring about a fairer and more balanced view of the Civil War. Among Professor Dodd's books in this field are "The Life of Jefferson Davis," "Statesmen of the Old

South," and "The Cotton Kingdom." The last named book is one of the volumes in that very popular historical series, "The Chronicles of America."

Professor Dodd will speak to us of the problems of Lincoln as President during the Civil War, and particularly during the year 1864, under the title, "Lincoln's Last Struggle—Victory?":—Professor Dodd.

Lincoln's Last Struggle
—Victory?

By William E. Dodd

Professor of History, University of Chicago

Lincoln's Last Struggle —Victory?

"That government of the people for the people and by the people shall not perish from the earth."

I

IT WAS the third winter of the war.[1] Abraham Lincoln and Mary Todd were still in the White House. The doors of the fashionable capital, so long closed, opened now and then. The dean of Washington bankers, W. W. Corcoran, his slaves unwilling to abandon so noble a master, gave his first great reception, wild radicals of the new regime modestly elbowing their ways about. Then George Washington Riggs, not to be outdone, opened his "baronial estate and house," all the semi-secessionists there, Gideon Welles of the Cabinet duly received if not lionized. And Kate Chase, a marvel for the daughter of an abolitionist, now married to the master of mills in Rhode Island and an honored senator, gave dinners to match those of the former wonder-working Mrs. Clement C. Clay, Paris gowns and crinolines looking

[1]Professor B. Smith Haworth, The High School, Ottawa, Kansas, has assisted me greatly in the location and amplification of references and quotations, for which I desire to make thankful acknowledgment.

William E. Dodd

as handsome on the figures of rich New Englanders as they had formerly looked on the slender mistresses of plantations. Nor did Mrs. Lincoln really milk her cow on the White House lawn every evening at twilight. Gentle Washington, abandoning hope that Lee would ever return in force, learned to look upon life with a little more of indulgence.

The years had been long and dreary, and Lincoln's political family had grown used to their unwonted tasks, though they did not exactly love their chief. Henry Halleck, a thick-headed translator of the famous Jomini, never a battle to his credit, was chief of staff, a vain, pretentious strategist too incompetent to be retained, too powerful to be dismissed, was ever at hand—teaching Lincoln the game of kings. Edwin M. Stanton, bald, ill-tempered and blustering, at loggerheads with half the generals in the field and distrustful of the rest, the "American Carnot" marshalling the forces of an unmilitary people and keeping close counsels with the President's enemies, was Secretary of War and contemptuous of Lincoln. If Halleck or Stanton failed the President, Salmon P. Chase, unruffled and complacent, the Secretary of the Treasury, improviser of loans that ran into the billions and sponsor for hundreds of millions of doubtful greenbacks, Salmon P. Chase, intriguing by day and by night to supplant the Illinois lawyer whom "mere accident" had elevated to exalted station. The various groups, who for political advantage, had stormed the "Willard" and harassed the President-elect up to the very night preceding the inauguration, had never become reconciled to the fact that the Cabinet contained men of all factions and faiths. The senatorial bloc who tried to take over the management of the Cabinet in 1862, were hoping to complete that task in the fullness of time, and if the President himself should be compelled to resign, so much the better. They had been foiled by the political astuteness of the President once, but they had not despaired of a better day. So with a Washington grown a little more friendly and a cabinet as little united as ever, Lincoln faced the unfriendly congress that his emancipation proclamation had done much to give him.

Congress had assembled on the seventh of December, Charles Sumner unforgiving and magisterial, was the chief of all the senators, Benjamin F. Wade, his sawed-off gun now at home in Ohio, chairman of the committee on the conduct of the war, worshipful follower—other commanding figures of that body: Lyman Trumbull, the upright, John P. Hale, the fault-finder and Zachary Chandler, brusk and ruthless egotist, all bent upon purging a backslidden country of all its mortal sins. In the house of representatives, Thaddeus Stevens, the weight of years and the plague of disease upon him, was master, a master of driving temper and relentless soul, an avowed enemy of Lincoln. Of equal importance was the young and handsome Henry Winter Davis of Maryland, a former slaveholder, now the scourge of all slaveholders, an ally of Stevens, a disappointed aspirant for the seat in the President's cabinet held by another Marylander, Montgomery Blair. Two of the most tragic figures of all that tragic time. Lincoln had won the battle of Gettysburg. Would he win in the impending struggle with congress?

On the first day of the session the President endeavored to secure a friendly speaker. Thaddeus Stevens and Winter Davis, perceiving the move, turned from their former candidate, Galusha A. Grow, to Schuyler Colfax, a westerner, and beat the President's western candidate on a big margin—defeat. On the eighth, the Louisiana plan of reconstruction, designed to make the southern return to the Union easier, a measure intended to bring about gradual emancipation and the earliest possible restoration of peace to the country,[1] was read to both houses, a proclamation issuing to the people at the same time. Members of congress restrained for a few days the wrath that observant men saw on many faces that day.

[1]Springfield *Republican,* quoted in *The National Intelligencer,* December 1864; Frank P. Blair, Lincoln's spokesman, in the house of representatives April 23, 1864.

This announcement of policy added to the latent opposition to the President that had been increasing with the passing of the weeks and months. "Visitors to Washington in '63 and '64 were struck with the lack of personal loyalty to him. . . They found few senators and representatives who would maintain cordially and positively that he combined the qualifications of leader in the great crisis."[1] What must have been Lincoln's thoughts, if he read the Congressional Globe and the utterances of such men as Wickliffe of Kentucky? "Thank God the people have been awakened by the many extraordinary arrests and wrongs committed on their fellow citizens," said Wickliffe early in the session. "They have spoken in terms of thunder. They should be obeyed by their servants." White, of Ohio, was no less vehement in declaring, "I owe no allegiance to Mr. Lincoln. I owe no allegiance to his cabinet-ministers." He thought only one man in all the world was more hated in Ohio than Lincoln, and that man, the governor of the state, was so hated because he supported Lincoln's policies.[2] Lincoln read enough to know a little of what lay ahead. Nevertheless he meant to guide the process of reconstruction in all the war-stricken region and allow no vindictive policy to prevail. Stevens and Davis, Sum-

---

[1] Edward L. Pierce, *Memoir and Letters of Charles Sumner.* IV, 194.
[2] *Cong. Globe.* 37th Cong. 3rd Sess. These and similar expressions throughout the session.

ner and Wade, Chase and Stanton were of another mind. They would take no dictation from any President. Would they take it from Robert E. Lee?

Lest the latter alternative ensue, Lincoln laid his careful and generous plan: he must win a military victory in spite of an unfriendly congress; he must win a military victory against Lee; and then he must secure his own re-election.

II

A serious programme, so much waiting upon circumstance. When Congress finished its organization, the great committees manned by opponents of the President, the Republicans organized a Republican National Executive Committee, the earnest and upright Samuel C. Pomeroy of Massachusetts and Kansas, the chairman, Wade and Sumner, Stevens and Davis godfathers to the plan. The young and hopeful James A. Garfield of the pious Western Reserve wrote home:[1] "We hope we may not be compelled to push Lincoln four years more." It was the business of the committee to push the Secretary of the Treasury, and the work of the succeeding campaign began in a brisk, bustling manner, little concern felt as to the consequences to a country torn by civil war. Horace Greeley, author of the cry "on to Richmond" in 1861 but none the wiser, still editor of the greatest news-

[1] T. C. Smith, *Life and Letters of James A. Garfield.* I, 375.

paper in the country, the New York *Tribune,* declared: "Lincoln's renomination means the revival of
the fear that the disasters, the burdens, the debts and
the hopes deferred will be revived." Theodore Tilton,
editor of the *Independent,* known far and near as the
organ of Henry Ward Beecher, urged:[1]

> "The ship of state tosses upon a rough sea; who
> shall take the helm? A nation tired of war will
> submit to be duped for the sake of peace. Great
> statesmen are few in any country, but few as they
> are we must make diligent search to find one for
> the next presidency."

There was no mistaking the language of the proph-
ets of Brooklyn. The sincere, if radical, Adam Gurowski, voiced the opinion of many another when he wrote,
"if Mr. Lincoln is re-elected, then self government is
not yet founded on reason, intellect and on sound
judgment."[2] On another occasion Gurowski wrote, "I
often meet Mr. Lincoln on the streets. He looks ex-
hausted, careworn, spiritless, extinct. I pity him!
. . .   That is the price for greatness to which he is
not equal. Yet, Mr. Lincoln, they say, wishes to be
re-elected!"[3] The New York *Evening Post,* one of its
managers, a son-in-law of William Cullen Bryant,

[1]*The Independent.* Feby. 18, 1864.   [3]*Ibid.,* 242.
[2]Adam Gurowski, *Diary.* II, 237.

prosecuted under the direction of the honest if indiscreet, Secretary of the Navy for gross frauds upon the Government, made earnest protest against the hasty and ill-advised renomination of so weak a leader as Lincoln.[1] The young and enthusiastic Whitelaw Reid of the Cincinnati *Gazette* prepared the ways for Chase in Ohio and the Middle West and sought to undo the vacillating President, about to "surrender the cause of human freedom to the masters of slave plantations." The New York *Herald,* always clever, threw itself whole heartedly into the anti-Lincoln crusade. This paper called upon all anti-Lincoln Republicans to demand a postponement of the Convention which Lincoln's opponents feared would be called too early for their effective resistance to his candidacy. Lincoln was "consistent in nothing, except in the role of a trifling joker," said the *Herald.* "He has been tried and proved a failure. . . His administration has thus been a broad and continuous farce."[2] As early as March this same paper had declared that opposed to Lincoln was "the great mass that condemn his war policy, his manifold blunders as chief executive officer of the nation, and are disgusted with his transparent unfitness for the responsible position he holds."[3] The Independent gave its emphasis to the

[1] Quoted in *The National Intelligencer,* March 10, 1864.
[2] The New York *Herald,* April 7, 1864.
[3] *Ibid,* March 16, 1864.

idea that Lincoln was sure to meet defeat in November, as matters stood in May and June. So nervous was this journal, that it thought no candidate should be nominated before September, inasmuch as fickle popularity might so waver in the hectic summer months, as to make the chance of any Republican doubtful. The idea was to wait so long to nominate that there would be little chance for unpopularity to assert itself. "If the Baltimore Convention had not office holders for members," complained the *Independent,* when the Convention had been called, "its managers would have yielded before this time to the popular wish for a postponement."[1] To all of this, as has already been indicated, the *Tribune* added a daily portion. On the very eve of the Convention, Greeley insisted it was no time to be thinking of elections. "We propose to act with the great body of our fellow unionists in the approaching canvass," the *Tribune* managed to say, but inasmuch as Lincoln seemed to be in a fair way to receive the nomination, the paper was, to use its words, "in no hurry to enter upon that canvass."[2] So as one turns today the fragile pages of the leading newspapers of that time, the conclusion becomes irresistible that the wise, the rich and the good were sick and tired of Abraham

[1]*The Independent,* June 6, 1864.

[2]The New York *Tribune,* June 6, 1864.

Lincoln, just then calling for five hundred thousand more young men, young men to be drawn from the homes of farmers and workers, if not from those of greater folk who furnished substitutes at three or four hundred dollars apiece.

And this disgust with the President gave easy access to the scores and hundreds of agents of the treasury department to talk the cause of Chase and suggest the strange alliance of prosperous eastern business men, making forty percent a year, and the political abolitionists. Benjamin F. Wade was as enthusiastic as his own ambition would allow; Winter Davis of Baltimore shouted for the Secretary of the Treasury; Secretary Stanton gave secret assurance, I think, of his potent aid; Chase clubs sprang up overnight in the cities and towns of the country—the Secretary himself absent more and more from cabinet meetings. On February 20 the hopeful Pomeroy published the confidential circular which had been in newspaper offices for some time. The main points of this document were: Lincoln can not be re-elected; if he were re-elected, he would ruin the country with his flagrant corruptions and his weak compromises with the slaveholders.[1] This was not the language of a narrow-minded party boss. It came from the head of the treasury, a man who had long been known as

[1] The New York *Herald*, February 23, 1864.

one of the great leaders of the country. Lincoln must bestir himself, the sluggish Lincoln.

He was not unready, nor without clever supporters. William H. Seward, older and wiser, abandoning forever the ambition of a tortuous career, was already laying wires all over New York; and Thurlow Weed, forgetting an earlier remark that "imbecility was supreme in Washington," partner in many a midnight contrivance, was ready for a new assignment, that Thurlow Weed who had denied Henry Clay the presidency twenty-four years before, his hands now as ever upon the Whig business men of New York. The wiry Seward and the easy-spoken Weed made a pair it were well to have on one's side. Nor was the young, pushing Henry J. Raymond, editor of the New York *Times,* though earlier in the administration often halfhearted, without great influence. Outside the realm of party organization, there was Samuel Bowles, a man of clear vision and honest purposes, editor and maker of the Springfield *Republican,* supporting Lincoln against Sumner, and boldly declaring that the Louisiana plan meant gradual and reasonable abolition of slavery. Interesting protagonists, these, but a more interesting group was the race of Blairs, now almost unknown to history: "Old Frank" Blair, who had laid many an intrigue for Andrew Jackson, living now in a great mansion there at Silver Spring, Maryland, a tall Kentuckian, oracular, unscrupulous, accomplished, slipping in and out of the White House at all hours of the day or night, ardent champion of the backwoods lawyer from Illinois, and not without reason: his son, Montgomery Blair, the Postmaster General in Lincoln's cabinet, a tall, angular man of broad forehead and narrow shoulders, tight-drawn mouth and solemn visage, a fire-eater of 1861, chiding Lincoln for dickering at all with the rebels at Charleston, a deadly enemy of Winter Davis, the other boss of Maryland, was ready to make hasty work of Chase, his colleague, and all opponents of the President. Two interesting Blairs. There was another, Frank Blair, the younger, who had "saved Missouri" to the Union in 1861, a West Pointer, a general in the army of Tennessee and a member of Congress from Saint Louis at the same time, choosing to sit in the house that stormy winter, his commission wisely deposited in a secret drawer in the White House. All the Blairs, owners of slaves, organizers of Lincoln support in Maryland, in Kentucky and Missouri, gradual emancipationists, heirs of the Jackson tradition, were enlisted in the war for Lincoln; Chase and Davis, Stanton and Stevens making grimaces the while. But there was yet another member of the family, Gustavus Vasa Fox, son-in-law of the great house at Silver Spring, Assistant Secretary of the Navy, a Massa-

chusetts man, tied up, as became men of that great
state, with mills and industry, trained at Annapolis
and not without money in his purse, giving orders to
the bearded, wise-looking Secretary of the Navy,
whose *Diary* was slipped into a drawer as you entered
the big room; he was not less a Lincoln man than the
strenuous general in the house of representatives. And
Lincoln himself held leaders like Joseph Medill of
the Chicago *Tribune* firmly to his interest and drew
into the camp the marvellous preacher-orator, Robert
J. Breckinridge, a son in the Confederate army and
an uncle in command of rebel regiments in the valley
of Virginia, as much a master of the shorter and the
longer catechisms as Wade himself, one who was to
do valiant service in the convention at Baltimore. It
was not a weak combination, barring the absence of
the abolitionists—the masses of inarticulate people
coming more and more to have faith in the harassed
President.

The opening gun of the administration was an
article by James Russell Lowell, author of the *Bige-
low Papers,* "the apostle of culture" as James Ford
Rhodes of the ponderous history was wont to say.
Lowell wrote so vigorous a defense of Lincoln in the
North American Review, that the weak defenders
who had dared run counter to the general trend up to
that time, were themselves astonished. The *Review*

pointed out that Lincoln was in no sense the failure his opponents tried to make him out to be. He had given the war steady purpose and definite aim; even the New York *Times,* as hopeful as any part of the Lincoln press, had never dared say that. The article maintained also that Lincoln had "made popular excitement into earnest national will, moral sentiment into a practical moral end, and treason of enemies, unwise zeal of friends and jealousy of rivals had been made useful for good." Nor did the article overlook the fact that Lincoln had prevented a foreign war. All this, Lowell said, was due to the "good sense, good humor, sagacity, large mindedness, and unselfish honesty of the unknown man whom a blind fortune, as it seemed, had lifted from the crowd to the most dangerous and difficult eminence of modern times." Having begun so able a defense, the writer was not content until he had predicted that "history will regard Mr. Lincoln as among the most prudent of statesmen and the most successful of rulers."[1] History once again was playing strange tricks, making doubtful prophecy, if not mere guess-work, into established wisdom.

It was encouraging to have so wise a man of the East say in the *North American Review* more than you could say yourself. Lincoln read the pronounce-

[1] *North American Review,* January 1864. 234-60.

ment twice, wondering whether he could be so great
a statesman as was there portrayed. Nevertheless, ob-
livious of the barrage of newspaper opposition in
other quarters, such support gave impetus for more
active moves.   Edwin D. Morgan of New York, a
great merchant who was able a little later to give away
a million dollars, called the Republican National committee to meet on Washington's birthday in Washington, Gideon Welles of the cabinet sitting with
them. They read the Pomeroy circular, just then under discussion in the press, but said nothing fit to
print;[1] they resolved themselves into the National
Union Republican committee and called the next Republican National convention to meet in Baltimore as
the National Union Republican convention on June 7,
three weeks later than the convention which first nominated Lincoln had assembled. But the Chase men re-
doubled the cry of "premature" and Winter Davis
hurried over to Baltimore and engaged the only available hall for the week of June 7 and put the keys in
his pocket. Nearly all the Republicans in congress
were still for Chase and all the papers in New York
but two continued to be opposed to Lincoln, if not
in favor of Chase; but on the fifth of March the Union
Republican caucus of the Ohio legislature had met
and declined to endorse Chase, the "favorite son."

[1]Gideon Welles, *Diary* I, 529.

Lincoln had won on two counts: the National committee favored his renomination and the Union Republican party of the greatest western state seconded the National committee, though Lincoln's own state was in serious doubt. Chase withdrew from the canvass, though he by no means ceased to fight what he called the "sly Illinoisian."

Lincoln was hardly content with the outlook, the great states of Pennsylvania and Massachusetts hostile to him. The spring was opening and military successes in order, successes which few expected. There must be a majority in Baltimore, even if Davis did not let them have the convention hall; and he unfolded his plan. Michael Hahn of Louisiana must hasten the organization of the new Louisiana, not forgetting the delegates to Baltimore; John Hay slipped off to Florida to make a state out of two counties, held by the army, and lead its delegation to the Union Republican convention; John Steele of Arkansas was to superintend similar work in Arkansas; and Parson Brownlow of eastern Tennessee, who needed no prodding, would bring up the delegates from that bewildered community. In western Virginia the President's agents were teaching former slaveholders the rubrics of new and unaccustomed roles. If New Englanders and Horace Greeley, Salmon P. Chase and the irreconcilables in the senate and house would insist upon a bitter fight, Lincoln would present them with delegations from the border states and enthusiastic supporters from the "ten per cent" communities of the South, not to mention Robert J. Breckinridge and Parson Brownlow.

Although Chase withdrew early in April, the course of events in congress ran steadily against the President and Lincoln's friends endeavored to reply. Frank Blair was set up or set himself up to speak for the Administration. On February 27, he gave distinct warning what he might say; but on April 23, he rose again, his general's commission still in Lincoln's possession, epaulets upon his manly shoulders, the proud father safe, I think, in the galleries and began the most sensational speech that had been made in congress since Charles Sumner indicted a whole people in the *Barbarism of Slavery*. The Secretary of the Treasury was the butt of the driving, if not ferocious attack: Chase had squandered the hard-earned money of the people to advance his precious candidacy; he had sent out hundreds of clever cotton traders with Treasury permits to finance the Pomeroy business; then Blair read a letter from a great New York banker which declared that Chase had given his son-in-law, Senator Sprague, a permit to buy cotton enough to make him two million dollars; and the Secretary even maintained corrupt gangs of radicals in

Missouri and Maryland to break down the power of the chief who had made him. Any gentleman would resign his place in the cabinet when he thus set up to attack his chief. The house was in an uproar; senators, learning of the attack, were indignant; and the newspapers outside at once made a sensation[1]—it was Abraham Lincoln reduced to the necessity of fighting, fighting through a Blair, Seward, Welles and Bates rejoicing.

Had Lincoln read the speech? Did he direct such an onslaught from a seat in the house against a member of his cabinet? All the world asked these questions. The president was embarrassed, his general having overshot the mark; but some of the charges of corruption leveled by Chase's agents against the Administration were answered. The leaders of the house called for an immediate investigation. Lincoln returned Blair his commission, raised him to the command of the 17th army corps and hastened him off to Sherman, and seemed not a little pleased at the anger and demoralization of all his enemies, Chase and Stanton keeping discreetly away from cabinet sessions. There were no satisfactory answers to Blair's attack, James A. Garfield, prospective successor to the wrathful Joshua Giddings, wrote sorrowfully again to his wife: "Lincoln will be nominated and a copperhead

[1]Gideon Welles, *Diary* II, 20.

will be elected. Not a dozen men in congress think otherwise."[1] A discouraging prospect naturally followed by other gloomy forebodings.

Sumner was no less of the opinion than before that Lincoln was "wanting in the style, in the gravity of manner and of conversation, which are becoming the chief of a nation." "In capacity and temperament," he thought, "he was inadequate to the responsibilities of the head of a nation at such a momentous period." Andrew, of Massachusetts, too, more or less the voice of all New England, never reconciled to Lincoln's interference in behalf of the unscrupulous Ben Butler *in re* the Massachusetts enlistments in 1862, interpreted Lincoln as above all a politician, and thought if the country were saved it would be "in spite of him, and not because of him."[2] When the Administration, in punishment for the publication of a forged proclamation, suspended the New York *World* late in May, the usual troublesome but soft voiced *Independent,* called the government to account as a "many-headed author of hallucinations, a spinner of false prophecies, a rainbow-painter of delusive hopes and ninety-day wonders."[3] If such expressions are representative of loyal sentiment, what must have been the vehemence

[1] T. C. Smith, *Life and Letters of James A. Garfield.* I, 376.
[2] H. G. Pearson, *John A. Andrew,* II, 150.
[3] May 26, 1864.

of the opposition, otherwise known as the "copper-head" press? All in all, the Garfield prophecy was not wide of the mark as things stood.

III

The call of the battlefield pressed by day and by night. Lee and his praying ironsides waited there on the half-barren ridges south of the Wilderness; Joseph E. Johnston of the bald head and snuff-brown face, sixty thousand veterans about him, there on the hills of northern Georgia, waiting for the onset of Sherman and his hardened farmers. The gentle Lincoln, dreading the inevitable slaughter, permitted the elder Blair to slip off to Richmond and say to Jefferson Davis: "If you will let me write a re-united country into any agreement, you may write the rest."[1] Davis, hardening his heart, after the manner of the Pharoes, declared there could never be a return to the Union. And Lincoln had to continue his vast preparations for the struggle, looking the while for a general to take the place of doubting Meade. The Blairs, always clever, suggested McClellan and opened correspondence with "copperheads" to that end.

The young Napoleon, more popular every day than the preceding, could hardly promise what Blair asked: i. e. not to think of running for the presidency against

[1] I have paraphrased and condensed the message. See J. F. Rhodes, *History of the United States*, V, 59.

Lincoln. That was about all McClellan thought of day or night that winter. Had not Stanton delayed and delayed the official report of military operations in 1861 and 1862 in the hope of weakening the general's candidacy, a report which declared to the world:[1]

> "This war should not look to subjugate states; it should not be a war upon the southern population; there should be no confiscations of property, no political executions, no forcible abolition of slavery."

Had not Lincoln done all these things? The report came out early in the winter, ten thousand copies printed for the special benefit of members of congress. The New York *Herald* thought it contained weighty matter and wise policy. Horace Greeley, opponent of Lincoln that he was, said: "General McClellan is the Pro-Slavery candidate and he will prove more formidable in the canvass than in the field." McClellan was indeed the candidate and none had done more to give him a following than Lincoln himself, when at the behest of Stanton, he had dismissed him from the command of the army of the Potomac, the day after the last national election. On March 18, there was a

---

[1] The New York *Tribune*, Jan. 7, 1864. I have compressed a paragraph of McClellan's famous letter of July 7, 1862.

"monster" mass meeting in Cooper Institute, New York; the aged Amos Kendall, of the Jackson kitchen cabinet, presided and talked of the great general of the day and of the greater general of old time who was of the same mind. It was clear that the young Napoleon could not be made the commander to try fortunes once more with Lee. But who was to be chosen to the unenviable task?

General W. S. Rosecrans of Ohio, who had been approached by Horace Greeley to become a candidate against Lincoln, had ruined himself at Chattanooga; General George H. Thomas, the hero of Chickamauga, was a Virginian; and William Tecumseh Sherman, brother of the suave, cautious senator from Ohio, of sharp and profane speech, was "crazy." There was no other than the little Ulysses S. Grant, disliked of Halleck and feared by Stanton, a West Pointer, too, and a commander with a record for "slaughtering" his men. It was a strange fate that made the son of a hard-boiled Democrat, tanner Jesse Grant of southern Ohio, the son-in-law of Colonel Frederick Dent, a shouting Democrat of Missouri and a slaveholder of positive views, the only available man to beat Lee, Mrs. Grant the owner of slaves, having hired them out for her own most needful support a year or two before. But war and politics make strange bed-fellows. There must be a new commander of the army of the Potomac, five hundred thousand hesitating volunteers and conscripts slowly gathering under the unwelcome call of February 1, gathering at a score of training camps in New York, Pennsylvania, Ohio, Indiana and the rest of the doubtful states. Time and tide would not wait that anxious winter.

The burly Stanton had gone to Louisville a little before congress assembled, a train all to himself, to see and talk with Grant. The Secretary and the General, none too friendly, met in a private room; they talked one knows not what; they were to meet again at eight o'clock in the evening. The hour arrived, but there was no General Grant. The irascible and self-centered Secretary paced the floor of his room; he sent out hasty agents to seek the indifferent Grant, not to be found on street or alley. At eleven in the evening, the hero of Vicksburg appeared. He had been found, Stanton's intimate friend, Don Piatt, said at a place and in a condition not to be mentioned in a public report. How could Stanton recommend such a man, a Democrat and a slave holder too? Did the re-union of a great country turn upon the answer to this two-sided question?

Lincoln pondered, made inquiries and told some of his uneasy conscience keepers that he would like to get a little of the liquor the General drank—it seemed to make him fight. But would the general take the command of all the armies, win a great battle and then, like McClellan, set up for Democratic candidate? The presidential bee was abroad, the New York *Herald* already advocating Grant for the Democratic nomination![1] Scarcely an issue of the paper but had its front-page as well as its editorial appeal. And the influence of its propaganda seemed to be far reaching. At least the *Herald* thought so. "From all parts of the country," the paper reported as early as January, "do we continue to receive proofs of the growing sentiment of the people in favor of the election of General Grant." The movement, if the clever New York daily had its way, was sure to become a stampede as soon as those with "ulterior motives" could see the handwriting on the wall. The extent of corruption became a favorite theme. If Lincoln himself were honest, the *Herald* was bold enough to say, "it was because he was too imbecile to be otherwise." As to politics, it thought Lincoln the "most dishonest politician who ever went to Washington."[2] Sooner or later, all sensible people would see that Grant was the remedy. How far from the mark this prediction was, of course, no one could then know.

Horace Greeley, too, the busy-body, had sent John R. Gilmore, the propagandist, to tempt Grant into

[1] The New York *Herald,* April 27, and earlier.
[2] January 13, 1864.

the Republican fold with the suggestion of the presidency. It was not a light matter, Lincoln's great cause seeming to depend on the whims or the ambitions of mere men. Then Lincoln learned that Grant's most intimate friend in Chicago, J. R. Jones, a busy, money-making man, might know what was under Grant's hat. Lincoln sent for Jones, and Jones, as he was leaving Chicago, took a letter from the post office. It was from the stodgy General at Chattanooga, who reported that politicians pestered him about the White House. He had no patience with such. He was a fighting man. The letter safe in an inside pocket, Jones appeared at the White House, Lincoln ruminating, walking about the room, his wrinkled face unrelieved. Surmising the cause, the visitor handed the President the precious letter. Lincoln's face eased, then it lighted up. "I like that kind of a general." The problem was solved.[1]

On the first of March Ulysses S. Grant was made commander in chief of all the armies, his own role to lead the attack upon Lee—it was no easy prospect, the little, stoopy general from the West, his coat unbuttoned, his cap over his eyes, his boots none too clean, silent, meditative, his unlucky past sometimes pestering him, father-in-law Dent always about and father Grant not unwilling to supply the army with

[1] Hamlin Garland, *Ulysses S. Grant.*

leather; but it was General Grant, nevertheless, "Unconditional Surrender," his motto. Lee knew quickly of the appointment, Lee who had dismissed a long series of Union commanders: McDowell and McClellan; Pope and McClellan again; poor Burnside and the bewildered Hooker; and then Meade who had won a victory without intending it. Now it was Grant "who would fight." Would it be the last? As I read history, the chances were with Lee that spring and not with the courageous new commander of the army of the Potomac. Grant said he was not a strategist, he did not study Jomini, the master; he did not care a great deal about topography—a dangerous frame of mind, if Grant represented himself aright that spring. It was March, the country doubtful, troubled, congress in a bad humor, though the senate confirmed the appointment. The roads began to dry; and Lincoln issued a call for two hundred thousand more men on the first of April, all the hospitals in Washington, Baltimore and Philadelphia providing more space and more beds, thousands and thousands of beds. Lincoln had entered upon the war for the Union; he could not retreat, his democracy "here and all over the world" at stake. As the day of encounter approached, the grapevine telegraph told Lincoln, cleverest of interpreters, that the people were tired of the long bloodshed, opposed to the repeated calls for soldiers; the wages of mill-workers were high and the workers were in a mood to resist the draft. Moreover, the credit of the Government declined every week, despite the efforts of Jay Cooke, his drives and his expensive advertising. Horace Greeley indicated that feeling when he wrote:[1]

"Why should not any man lend to his Government? If you have $1,000 in greenbacks, you get five per cent interest in gold and a gold bond, 48 per cent on the currency loaned. If you have $1,000 in specie, you can get $1,600 in greenbacks, lend it to the Government and receive $80 a year interest in gold and $1,600 principal when your bond falls due. Who can ask of his country better terms?"

IV

Grant made ready to strike: David Hunter was in the valley of Virginia, laying waste that fruitful source of Confederate supplies; Benjamin F. Butler threatened from Norfolk with forty thousand troops; Sherman had near a hundred thousand men in front of Johnston at Dalton, Georgia, and Grant himself was ready to cross the Rapidan—a vast complex of moves and maneuvers all under the direction of the chief of the Potomac. On the 4th of May, Grant

[1] *The Independent,* April 21, 1864.

crossed the river, marching southeast in the midst of the ghostly Wilderness, the bones of countless men and horses scattered about or protruding from shallow graves, the skeletons of last year's conflict grinning at the beginners of another desperate attack upon the South. On the 5th Lee struck at Grant's right flank with all the weight and drive of a Frederick II, regiments and divisions shrieking the famous Confederate yell as they emerged from the Wilderness which had screened them. Grant had never felt such a blow and his army was in a position where it could neither use its heavy artillery nor employ all its force. By the middle of the day, the Union cause seemed desperate and Grant thought of retreat as he threw himself, in a paroxysm of fear and excitement, upon his camp bed, a dangerous retreat, and posted regiments to hold the way open; Lee anticipating such a move, had hastened men to bar the way of retreat. A little later the Union commander observed that the momentum of Lee's attack was waning. Longstreet had taken the wrong road, Longstreet behind again, the battle could not be finished that day. On the morrow Grant was safe, but he lost eighteen thousand men.

Two days later Grant moved again toward Spotsylvania court house, on the way to Richmond. On the ninth Lee met the Union troops there and from that day till the eighteenth of May there were desperate encounters, Grant losing again twelve to fifteen thousand men, dead, wounded and missing. Gideon Welles says he went down the Potomac one day consumed with anxiety, and met great fleets of transports bringing the wounded and the prominent dead from the battlefields, other transports carrying fresh recruits to fill the gaps in the Union lines.[1] But neither Lincoln nor Grant could delay. On May 19 Grant moved toward Cold Harbor on the North Anna where he fell upon Lee again with the weight of half his army. He lost twelve thousand men in half an hour! It was June 2; vague and disturbing rumors spreading over the North: the Associated Press announcing merely "Heavy fighting in the Wilderness, three hundred and twenty five men killed at Cold Harbor."

Grant was in doubt, his men angry, some of his ablest generals protesting. The stock market tumbled in spite of assurances from Washington, tumbled till greenbacks were not worth forty cents in the hundred. The Union National Republican convention was gathering in Baltimore, Thurlow Weed doing what he could to hold the "wild men" in check, the men who would defeat Lincoln and at the same time issue a challenge to the French emperor, just then setting

[1]Gideon Welles, *Diary*, II, 32.

up the government of Maximilian in Mexico. The
country could not stand the news from the front. It
was not given. Lincoln was uneasy, his cabinet still at
loggerheads. It was a bad moment for a convention.
By a clever move Robert J. Breckinridge was designated to make the keynote speech; he proved a past
master, lifting men out of their despairing moods.
This tall slender southerner with eyes peering from
heavy overhanging brows, fairly electrified the crowd
of doubting, jealous delegates. "No government has
ever stood on irresistible foundations," he shouted,
"whose foundations were not built on traitor's blood.
It is a fearful truth, but we had as well know it at
once. Every blow you strike, and every rebel you kill,
and every battle you win, reluctant as we are to do it,
is adding a decade, it may be a century, it may be ten
centuries, to the perpetuity of your government, and
the freedom of your children."[1] To be sure, this was
not saying anything about Lincoln, but it had
masterful effect in diverting the attention of the convention from personal and more divisive projects, and
giving to it an atmosphere of militant crusade. Breckinridge went on to reannounce the Lincoln plan of
reconstruction. Governor William Dennison of Ohio
then re-echoed the moderate views of Lincoln when
he took the seat of chairman of the convention. The

[1] New York *Tribune* June 10, 1864.

President's southern delegations were there, arousing
the ire of Thaddeus Stevens who would have preferred
their scalps. Chase's friends were not without hope
that Lincoln would lose. The decision came when the
vote was taken on the seating of the Tennessee delegation, led by Parson Brownlow. The delegation was
at first denied a place. Then the Illinoisians reversed
their attitude, as Illinois has done since at critical
moments, and Lincoln became the master of the convention. The doubtful delegation was seated, other
southerners ready to take their places if needed. The
President was renominated without recorded opposition.[1]

When all was done, however, it can hardly be said
that any group was satisfied. The Blairs felt the convention was managed by the radicals, while Thaddeus
Stevens thought he had "lost at every point." He had
fought primarily against Lincoln's reconstruction
policy, and he had been outgeneraled by compromis-
ing southerners and the fiery uncouth Jim Lane of
Kansas. The New York *Herald,* manifestly unfriendly, thought "the whole affair looked like a
struggle of the delegates to obtain capital upon which
they could lay claim upon old Abe for a fat office."[2]

[1] There is a valuable article by Thurlow Weed in the *National Intelligencer,* after the crisis passed, which shows how difficult it was to keep
the anti-administration men in check.

[2] June 9, 1864.

At any rate, when Andrew Johnson, "Andy the tailor," the war democrat from Tennessee, was nominated for vice-president, so much more enthusiasm was given for him than for Lincoln, that it was noticeable enough. Lincoln himself heard of Johnson's nomination before he heard of his own, and wondered for a time, if all his carefully laid plans had gone awry.[1]

All the time the anti-Lincoln press was maintaining that the re-nomination of Lincoln was no fair index as to the tempo of the popular pulse. The *Independent* was not wrong when it said, "It is not to be denied that the outward and apparent unanimity for Mr. Lincoln gave no fair expression of the strong undercurrent of opposite sentiment existing in the minds of individual delegates."[2] It was a case where the opposition, being divided, could not make its strength felt. Congressman Julian came away from the convention muttering to himself that not one in ten favored what all ten had done.[3] It was a Lincoln victory, nevertheless, the first of the three he must win that summer— the irreconcilables returning to their places in congress to renew their contest with Lincoln about reconstruction. As Julian said, not wishing to be uncomplimentary to himself, "Opposition to Lincoln was

[1]See New York *Independent,* June 16, 1864.
[2]June 16, 1864.
[3]Julian, *Recollections,* 243.

secretly cherished by many of the ablest and most patriotic men in the party."[1]

All eyes turned, if they had ever been averted, to the contest in Virginia. A dispatch of a reporter that fifteen thousand new beds had been placed in the Washington hospitals gave the public deep concern, and slowly more and more of the casualty lists were published. Grant was denounced as "Butcher Grant," as if the killing of men were not the business of war. There was a growing demand that Grant be removed —the Union army dared not attack again at once, fifty-four thousand men lost in a month, some men saying that Grant had left a heap of dead bodies all the way to the Rapidan. Grant paused and gave the country time to read the news from Georgia. There Union forces made slow but sure headway, though neither the officials at Washington nor the people at home seemed to grasp the meaning of Sherman's cautious work, Sherman already more than half-way to Atlanta—only fifteen or eighteen thousand men lost. But nothing overcame the deepening gloom of the people and the press. It was the common thing to direct all the discontent toward the White House. Lincoln was held to be the cause of every calamity. The Louisville Daily *Democrat,* representative of the Democratic and border state press, "held Lincoln re-

[1] *Ibid.,* 237.

sponsible for every life thrown away on fruitless battle fields," and considered the administration "responsible for every calamity of the war." The New York *World,* though always extreme, nevertheless voiced a common sentiment in making the President the recipient of its strongest condemnation. While one wonders at the audacity of it, still more abusive expressions appeared in foreign journals. *Frazer's Magazine,* at the touch of an American pen, as early as 1862, held "Abraham Lincoln responsible to humanity and humanity's God, for all the blood that has been shed in this unholy war—for every life and limb that has been lost, for every widow and orphan that has been bereft . . . and for all the unappreciable agonies of half a million of wounded and dying men." For four years, the long suffering Lincoln had thus been held up to abuse and scorn. How long, he must have wondered, how long?

V

It was the moment for a master stroke of Lee, by no means conquered. A strange inertia came upon him. He had been ill the preceding winter; after Spotsylvania he was again stricken, calling out upon his sick bed, "Grant must never pass us again, never." The illness of a general may be as fatal in war as the loss of an army. But I do not know that illness seriously affected Lee's movements that June. He surely miscalculated. Grant was his objective. Jefferson Davis warned him June 9 that Grant might try to move south of the James river. Crossing the river in the face of a powerful enemy was no small feat. Grant sent two regiments toward the river where he might be supposed to cross; Lee sent similar detachments to the same neighborhood and there was skirmishing and fighting. But at the moment Grant was turning his columns southeast toward White House where the Pamunkey becomes the York river. Thence the great army, with long trains of supplies, heavy guns and droves of cattle marched by long detour to the lower James, the twelfth to the fifteenth of June. On the latter day Grant began to cross the river at City Point; on the eighteenth his army was safe on the other side; Lee had not fired a gun—it was as great a feat as the move by which Grant had taken Vicksburg.

At the very moment that Grant made ready to change his base and cross the Potomac, Lee planned the expedition of Jubal Early and John C. Breckin- ridge against Washington. Early took his division from Lee's army on the 13th of June and made the spectacular attack from Rockville which cut off the capital from the rest of the North for a period of two days. Lee learned with surprise on June 18 that Grant was approaching Petersburg. The maneuvers and marches through northern Virginia by Early and Breckinridge that June and July were the useless price Lee paid for the escape of Grant. It was a fatal moment, though the people of the North were unaware of Grant's great success. If Lee had caught Grant in the act of crossing the James river the consequences must have been incalculable. The stars were beginning to point dimly to the ultimate success of Abraham Lincoln.[1]

But while Lee allowed Grant to escape, Winter Davis and Thaddeus Stevens pressed through congress the reconstruction bill on which President Johnston was to be wrecked a year and a half later: There was to be immediate emancipation of the slaves; a majority of southerners were to be compelled to take an ironclad oath before any delegates could be seated in congress; and the southern states were to be compelled to accept the thirteenth amendment to the constitution as a condition to any reconstruction at all— a drastic measure as compared with Lincoln's ten per cent plan. On the first of July Chase, still in harmony with the opposition in congress, offered his resignation. The President accepted it and Chase took his departure, leaving the Blairs unmolested. And the New York *Herald* at last found something to rejoice about.

[1] General E. P. Alexander, *Memoirs of a Confederate*, discusses this at length. Ch. XXI.

If only Welles and Stanton could be removed also, the Herald would see some glimmer of hope.[1] On the 4th the leaders of congress presented Lincoln with their bill. He refused to sign it, members of the house and senate making earnest and threatening protest.

The anti-slavery radicals, even before this, despairing of justice in Lincoln's half-way measures, and fearful of both the wrath of God and of men if justice remained longer neglected, met in Cleveland late in May and nominated John C. Fremont as the man of the hour. He had always been right, in their opinion, on slavery, and but for Lincoln's interference would have accomplished much by military proclamation, despite his chief's vacillating attitude. An admirable combination—both a prophet and a martyr. The "Martyr" himself, however, not so sure of victory as his followers professed to be, said he would rather be right than be president; but inasmuch as Lincoln's re-election would be fatal to the country, he would make the race to save the cause. He saw "no alternative but to organize against him (Lincoln) every element of conscientious opposition with a view to prevent the misfortunes of his re-election."[2]

And so the storm gathered from all directions. On

[1] July 3, 1864.
[2] New York *Herald* June 7, 1864.

the 28th of June there was an uproarious mass meeting in Cooper Institute, Lincoln's name jeered and hissed in ominous tones. Theodore Tilton, editor of *The Independent,* though not favoring the Fremont movement, nevertheless wishing the Baltimore convention had chosen some one besides Lincoln, shouted from the platform that Seward had been seen drunk at the recent Baltimore Sanitary Fair. What such a disclosure would do to help the party Tilton professed to favor, it is hard to say. Orestes Brown, associate of Wendell Phillips, confessed that he had voted for the President in 1860. Now any man "should vote to defeat Lincoln and the party of shoddy." In Maryland and Missouri and in the Middle West in general there was growing unrest, even neighborhood warfare. On the 8th of July Horace Greeley declared in *The Tribune* "there is danger of social convulsions; but courage, countrymen, it is but the darkness before dawn." At that moment Lincoln was calling for five hundred thousand men out of a population of twenty million, i. e. since February 1. And, as if to intensify the fears of the country, the President set the 4th of August for a day of national humiliation and prayer. It looked as if the renomination, which the *Independent* said was but a gift of the President to himself, would be the last of Lincoln's victories.

Meanwhile the Democrats had not been idle. In

the city of Peoria, Illinois, there was a monster peace demonstration, Lincoln blamed for all the ills of the time. The friendly Saint Louis *Democrat* uncovered what was thought to be a vast conspiracy of mid-western opponents of the war, Democrats and "copperheads" uniting to take possession of the state governments, take control of the coming Democratic National convention in Chicago and bring the war to an end. The story was worse than facts, but the facts were serious enough. On August 10 there was an open air meeting on Union Square, New York, a demonstration on behalf of General McClellan, the candidate of army officers in general as well as of conservative people in all the states. Hiram Ketchum and other prominent New York business men were listed as vice-presidents of the meeting. The *Evening Post* estimated the crowd at sixty thousand, the *Tribune* at thirty thousand. The *Herald* declared, "Old Abe had not a friend among the thousands present. The most casual mention of his name provoked the most unanimous manifestations of dislike and disgust." McClellan was undoubtedly the choice of the people for the presidency at that time.

Lincoln, watching from Washington with sorrowful eye the vast drift of opinion, wrote on the 23rd the remarkable note of resignation in favor of McClellan, in the event of expected success, and in curious fashion procured the signatures of all his cabinet:[1]

"This morning as for days past it seems exceedingly probable that this administration will not be re-elected. Then it will be my duty to so co-operate with the president-elect as to save the union between the election and the inaugural; as he will have secured the election on such ground that he cannot possibly save it afterward."

As if the cup of bitterness were not to be allowed to become empty, on the eighth of August the papers of the North carried the angry reply of Wade and Davis to his refusal to adopt the congress plan of reconstruction, as violent an attack upon the President as any of this generation has witnessed, calling the President's pocket veto a "blow at the friends of his administration, at the rights of humanity, and at the principle of republican government," and closing with the charge: "the President strides headlong toward the anarchy his proclamation of December inaugurated." Conventions met here and there asking both Lincoln and Fremont to withdraw, one in Ohio suggesting a national convention for September 22nd, to nominate a candidate who could win the election, the New York *Herald* telling the world "Old Abe must

[1]Nicolay and Hay: *Complete Works of Abraham Lincoln*, II, 568.

either decline or suffer ignominious defeat." Newspapers in general were everywhere giving vent to solemn warnings that Lincoln's re-election meant disaster. On the 18th the papers carried a story that Lincoln had proposed an armistice to Jefferson Davis— the first news of the secret maneuvers of John R. Gilmore and Horace Greeley seeking a means of ending the war, Lincoln not unwilling even then if southerners would but remain in the Union. In the midst of all this distress and gloom and lawlessness, the Democratic leaders assisted by their own and the independent press prepared for the greatest convention they had seen since the days of Jackson and Polk. Eminent men all over the North, business men of great means and the smaller folk of conservative tendencies, in conventions and in mass meetings, showed the strength of the ancient party. When the delegates met in Chicago on August 29, it was plain to all that the majority of the country sympathized with their efforts to compromise the difference between North and South, as indeed the reception of Lincoln's similar efforts had shown—was there to be a peace without victory?

The convention met. It nominated George B. McClellan on the first ballot and without opposition, the downright peace element of the convention very popular and very powerful. The last day of August, the

country was of the opinion that Lincoln had no chance;
Wade and Davis still agitating; Greeley and Chase
still complaining and hopeless. The New York editors,
Greeley, Godwin and Tilton had sent out letters to
loyal governors, if one could use the word in 1864, in
which three questions were asked: (1) Can Lincoln
be re-elected, (2) Can your state be carried for Lincoln? (3) Should there be another candidate? Other
letters of similar vein went to newspaper editors and
men in public life. Even conservatives like Andrew of
Massachusetts interpreted the replies as showing that
"the only hope was in a new candidate." Opposition
papers, sensing the opportunity, thought this movement showed Lincoln's friends were at last completely
disgusted with what the *Herald* called the "imbecili-
ties, blunders, corruptions and buffooneries that had
marked the administration." Finally a committee of
leading Republicans, young Whitelaw Reid of the
Cincinnati *Gazette,* Horace Greeley of the *Tribune*
and George Updyke of the National Union Republican Committee, having entered into tacit agreements
with some senators and other leaders of the party,
made formal demand for the withdrawal of Lincoln
from the ticket and for the further agreement to yield
to the calling of another Union Republican convention
late in September, a convention that was to follow the
suggestions already made and to nominate another

candidate. Lincoln considered carefully the distressing urge of these prominent people and agreed to withdraw in case a more promising candidate could be agreed upon. And to show how strong the pressure was I have only to state that Lincoln, always before able to withstand any pressure, and as late as July telling Stanton, "I propose continuing myself to be the judge as to when a member of the cabinet shall be dismissed," nevertheless dismissed from the cabinet on the first of September his loyal friend, Postmaster General Blair, in part to appease the wrath of Chase and his followers, Blair yielding gracefully to the unwilling request of the President. On September 1, 1864, Abraham Lincoln's personal popularity had reached its lowest ebb, his great cause in the greatest danger, newspapers almost silenced, not daring even to say, "this is no time to change presidents," military successes delayed and delayed till men thought the siege of Petersburg and Atlanta would drag on till after the election.[1]

VI

Now, one of the strange denouements of history occurred. Joseph E. Johnston, a slow man of the type of McClellan, slowly yielding ground to Sherman north of Atlanta had retreated to the outer environs

[1] J. F. Rhodes, *History of the United States,* IV, 518-519, understates the case.

of Atlanta by the middle of July. The people of
Georgia, like the people of the North, unable to real-
ize the meaning of military situations, were frantic.
They cried out to Jefferson Davis to give them a general who could win victories. Davis, sore pressed at
every point, not forgetful of the fussy, complaining
character of Johnston, listened to the appeal.[1] There
was a secret conference held in the house of James
Lyons in the suburbs of Richmond. The outcome was
the removal of Johnston on July 18—instead of the
slow, engineering defence and piecemeal attack, which
would probably prolong the siege till winter, there
was, in obedience to popular demand, now to be an
energetic drive upon Sherman's front. If it succeeded,
Lincoln would have no military success and carry few
states in the election of November. If it failed, Sherman would win Atlanta and Lincoln's election would
become fairly certain, the southerners themselves as-
sisting thus in their own undoing and in the solution
of the great problem of Abraham Lincoln and his
faithful minority.

John B. Hood, wounded in one leg, the other shot
off, a fiery militarist of the type of Jackson or Nathan
B. Forest took command before Atlanta and began
his valiant but losing strokes. It was the last day of

[1]H. J. Pearce, Benjamin H. Hill, *The Civil War and Reconstruction,*
as yet unpublished, shows the extent of Georgia discontent.

August, the Democratic convention just finishing its work, Lincoln just dismissing Montgomery Blair, Robert E. Lee guarding the interests of the confederacy at Petersburg. Hood made his last unsuccessful attack upon Sherman. Atlanta fell, Lincoln heard the welcome story only on the 4th of September. The end of the weary and doubtful summer had come. Lincoln was successful in the second of his tasks. He called the nation into the churches to give thanks for the deliverance. The proposed second Union Republican convention did not assemble, poor Chase had little more to say. Winter Davis went to Philadelphia and made a great speech on behalf of the maligned President, more favorable than he was able to do later, as it turned out—the weather was good, the October sun as bright as ever the suns of Thomas Jefferson had been. The son of Nancy Hanks had won one of the great victories of history, he would surely be re-elected.

Political leaders, so long his enemies, perceiving now his ultimate victory, changed slogans or became apologetic. John A. Andrew, conscience lulled a little, wrote to Forbes, "Since we must have Lincoln, then the men of motives and ideas must get into the lead, must elect him, get hold of the machine and run it themselves."[1] The country could be saved after all, if Lincoln could be made the figurehead he ought to be!

[1]H. G. Pearson, *John A. Andrew*, II, 166.

Poor Greeley, of the *Tribune,* fell in sorrowfully behind the Lincoln parade because he could see no hope for McClellan. "Now we do not regard Mr. Lincoln as a great man," he wrote, "yet no candid observer who knows both will pretend that General McClellan is his equal in ability." Greeley still thought a stronger opponent would have defeated Lincoln. The *Independent* began to publish letters emphasizing Lincoln's good qualities, as if to prepare the way for editorial support with better grace. And even the New York *Herald* admitted that Sherman's victory had made McClellan's nomination "not only worthless, but ruin for all his future." Winter Davis, lukewarm and unreconciled, told waiting audiences that the "worst man on our side is better than the best man on their side." "We will vote for Abraham Lincoln," he said on occasion, "because . . . even if we preferred another now, we cannot have him; if we desire a change, we cannot change without bringing ruin upon the republic!" Warming to the subject in a later speech he made bold to say, "and when gentlemen, the people have elected their president, they will let him know whatever his proclivities or disposition may be, whatever doubts may encumber or hang around his mind still, whatever his private opinions, they must be subordinated to the will of the American people."[1] Such

[1] Henry Winter Davis, *Speeches and Addresses,* 430 ff.

was the tortuous and tragic effort of an irreconcilable, trying to line up, but still unconvinced. Even so valiant a political supporter as William H. Seward could do no more than suggest that it was not Lincoln alone but what he represented that deserved support. "I therefore regard the pending presidential election," he said, "as involving the question, whether, hereafter we shall have our constitution and country left us."[1] Lincoln deserved the votes, not for what he was personally, but because his election had been the immediate cause of secession, was his argument.

The die-hards, however, were to play a more desperate game. They refused to see a Lincoln victory, possibly from sheer desire to prevent it. The New York *Herald* made a last appeal on the 28th of October. "Let the electors drop both McClellan and Lincoln," it urged, and using their technical constitutional privilege, elect General Grant. The *World,* on the other hand, kept up the fight for McClellan. Evidences that many thousands were of the same opinion are not entirely lacking. New York City witnessed a great McClellan meeting, almost on the very eve of election. Here Lincoln and his policies were flayed from every angle. When the votes were counted it was found New York City had favored McClellan by 30,000 votes, and in the country at large the Demo-

[1]Frederic Bancroft, *William H. Seward,* II, 408 citing *Works,* V, 496.

crats had polled the respectable total of 1,802,000. As to electors, of course, Lincoln had a tremendous majority, though electors, then as now, are hardly fair indices of popular opinion.

But Lincoln was still gentle, his thoughts turning more and more to his miserable southern fellow countrymen. In the annual message he recommended the passage of the thirteenth amendment and made plain that the southerners must accept it, but he did not talk the language of victors. In the second inaugural he said:

"Both the peoples of the North and the South read the same Bible and pray to the same God, and each invokes his aid against the other. It may seem strange any men should dare to ask a just God's assistance in wringing their bread from the sweat of other men's faces, but let us judge not that we be not judged. The prayers of both could not be answered. That of neither has been answered fully . . . With malice toward none, with charity for all, with firmness in the right as God gives us to see the right, let us strive to finish the work we are in."

There were many men of power in congress who liked not the language of their chief, the only man who could have saved the case for them, Stevens and Sumner and Davis—waiting for the moment to join

issues with the head of their own party, men unable
to rise to heights, men blinded by passion and fears,
interests and hatreds. Toward the end of March, the
forces of Robert E. Lee running low, Lincoln went
to City Point, Virginia, there to advise with Grant,
expectant of victory, and with Sherman, just closing
his spectacular march through the Carolinas, the
simple, modest, democratic chief of the great Northwest, giving law at last to the finest of all the aristo-
crats the old South had ever produced. Sumner was
with Lincoln, calling ever and anon for the blood of
the guilty; Lincoln replying, "judge not that ye be
not judged." The fighter of many and bitter battles
in congress unable to forgive, the pacifist trying to
make peace by the methods of war. Lincoln's terms
to the South were not severe; they were adequate. As
Lincoln turned his way back to Washington, Lee sur-
rendered with all the dignity that any victor might
have assumed. Grant bore himself with all the modesty
that greatness ever commands. It was not a bad day
for a nation that had much yet to do.

On the eleventh of April, the country rejoicing as
it never had rejoiced, never having come so near the
abyss before, some friendly serenaders called upon the
President. He spoke from a White House balcony:

"I am much censured for what I have done in
Louisiana. Whether the Southerners have ever

been out of the Union or not does not concern me. The Southerners finding themselves safely at home, it would be utterly immaterial whether they had ever been abroad. Let us all join in doing the acts necessary to restoring the Union, and forever after innocently indulge each his own opinion whether the Union was ever dissolved."

Three days later he added in the presence of his cabinet, poor Stanton present, I think:

"I hope there will be no persecution, no bloody work after the war is over. None need expect me to take part in hanging or killing men. We must extinguish our resentment if we expect to have harmony and union."

Was the chieftain who had run so stormy a course really victorious? Would his country rise to the levels of its far-seeing leader? There was a growing body and party of men and leaders making ready to say No, and to enter upon one of those contests which so often mar the pages of history, a conflict of animosities and interest not yet ended. But the hand of the assassin stayed the career of Abraham Lincoln. Mary Todd carried his remains home to the kindly neighbors of Springfield, where all the world journeys ever and anon to pay respect to one of its immortals.

OFFICERS AND DIRECTORS
SUSTAINING MEMBERS
CONTRIBUTORS TO ENDOWMENT

DIRECTORS

FRANK O. LOWDEN

GEORGE PASFIELD, JR.

LOGAN HAY

PASCAL E. HATCH

ARTHUR D. MACKIE

J. PAUL CLAYTON

HENRY M. MERRIAM

ALICE E. BUNN

EDWARD D. KEYS

GEORGE W. BUNN, JR.

HENRY A. CONVERSE

OFFICERS

LOGAN HAY, *President*

MARY E. HUMPHREY, *Vice-President*

J. H. HOLBROOK, *Treasurer*

GEORGE W. BUNN, JR., *Recording Secretary*

PAUL M. ANGLE, *Executive Secretary*

RESIDENT SUSTAINING MEMBERS

ABELS, HENRY
ANGLE, PAUL M.
ARMBRUSTER, JULIUS W.
ARMSTRONG, T. J.
ARMSTRONG, W. P.
ARMSTRONG, WILLIAM PRICE, JR.
BAINUM, NOAH C.
BAKER, H. B.
BANCK, HANS J. E.
BARBER, CLAYTON J.
BARBER, JOHN A.
BARKER, MORTON D.
BARKER, S. A.
BARNES, EDGAR S.
BARTHOLF, H. B.
BENGEL, GEORGE A.
BENGEL, HENRY G.
BERGER, H. W.
BERNARD, J. C.
BLACK, JOHN W.
BLACKSTOCK, IRA B.
BLACKSTOCK, MRS. IRA B.
BOOTH, ALFRED
BOWEN, A. L.
BRETSCHER, G. C.
BRETZ, JOHN E.
BRETZ, MRS. JOHN E.
BRETZ, J. F.
BRIGGLE, CHARLES G.
BRINKERHOFF, GEORGE M. JR.
BRINKERHOFF, GEORGE M. SR.
BROADWELL, STUART
BROADWELL, MRS. STUART
BROWN, A. C.
BROWN, MRS. A. C.
BROWN, JANE L.
BROWN, MRS. MARY EDWARDS
BROWN, MILTON HAY
BROWN, MRS. MILTON HAY
    *Deceased.

BROWN, OWSLEY
BROWN, VIRGINIA STUART
BUNN, ALICE EDWARDS
BUNN, GEORGE W. JR.
BUNN, MRS. GEORGE W. JR.
BUNN, GEORGE W. SR.
BUNN, MRS. GEORGE W. SR.
BUNN, HENRY
BUNN, HENRY II
BUNN, JACOB JR.
BUNN, MRS. MILDRED J.
BUNN, MILDRED J. II
BUNN, WILLARD
BURNETT, SAMUEL T.
BUTLER, A. MARIE
CALL, S. LEIGH
CAMPBELL, ERNEST J.
CANTRALL, E. E.
CARLSTROM, OSCAR E.
CATRON, B. L.
CATRON, MRS. B. L.
CHAPIN, E. L.
CHAPMAN, A. W.
CLAYTON, J. PAUL
CLAYTON, MRS. J. PAUL
CLENDENIN, GEORGE W.
*CLENDENIN, HENRY W.
COE, LAUREN W.
COE, LOUIS J.
COLEMAN, LOGAN
COLEMAN, LOUIS G.
COMPTON, C. W.
CONDELL, ELIZABETH B.
CONDELL, HELEN E.
CONDELL, THOMAS
CONKLING, MRS. CLINTON L.
CONVERSE, ALBERT E.
CONVERSE, HENRY A.
CONVERSE, MRS. W. O.

Cook, Mrs. John C.
Corneau, Addison
Currier, Mrs. Mary Priest
Davis, Henry
Diller, Isaac R.
Diller, William Hughes
Dines, C. S.
Dirksen, Theodore J.
Dixon, L. M.
Dixon, N. M.
Doyle, C. J.
Easley, James A.
Eckstein, Michael
Edmands, Charles H.
Emmerson, Louis L.
Enos, Allen
Evans, Frank N.
Farrington, Frank
Farris, Joseph
Fish, George A.
Fish, Mrs. George A.
Fisher, Leon E.
Funk, Donald S.
*George, John E.
George, Mrs. John E.
Giffin, D. Logan
Gillespie, Louis
Gingold, J. K.
Gotshall, R. W.
Gottschalk, Arthur
*Gottschalk, Fred
Graham, James M.
Griffin, James A.
Haas, R. W.
Hagler, Arthur L.
Hagler, Elmer E.
Hagler, Mrs. Elmer E.
Hall, Edward A.
Hammerslough, Joseph
Hatch, Ozias M.
Hatch, Mrs. Ozias M.
Hatch, Pascal E.

Hatch, Mrs. Pascal E.
Hatcher, O. W.
Hay, Logan
Hay, Mrs. Logan
Hay, Mary Douglass
Helmle, George B.
*Helmle, George H.
Hemmick, J. E.
Hereford, A. L.
Herndon, O. L.
Hill, H. B.
Hodgson, Charles F.
Hoff, Alonzo
Holbrook, J. H.
Holbrook, Mrs. J. H.
Holtz, Fred
Hoover, Wilber C.
House, Henry B.
Humphrey, Mary E.
Humphrey, Maude
Hurst, W. C.
Ide, Francis P.
Ide, Mrs. Francis P.
Ide, Roy W.
Irwin, Edward F.
Irwin, Horace C.
Irwin, Oramel B.
Jageman, W. M.
James, Paul
Jefferson, Roy T.
Jenks, C. E.
Jennings, Frank
Johnston, J. C.
Jones, Harry P.
Keys, Alvin S.
Keys, Edward D.
Keys, Mrs. Edward D.
Keys, Edward L.
Keys, George E.
Keys, Mrs. George E.
Klaholt, Carl H.
Klaholt, Harry F.

*Deceased.

KNUDSON, T. J.
KREIDER, MRS. EMMA
KREIDER, GEORGE P.
LANGE, B. A.
LANPHIER, GOIN
LANPHIER, JOHN
LANPHIER, ROBERT C.
LANPHIER, MRS. ROBERT C.
LESTER, MRS. A. J.
LEMMONS, W. H.
LEWIS, JOHN L.
LEWIS, MARY
LOMELINO, E. F.
LOONEY, J. D.
LOWE, FRANK H.
LUERS, B. H.
MACKIE, A. D.
MACPHERSON, MRS. EDNA O.
MALDANER, CHARLES J.
MATHENY, R. C. O.
MATHENY, ROBERT
McANULTY, R. H.
McCONNELL, WILL H.
McDONALD, DUNCAN
McKOWN, ROY Z.
McPHERSON, H. W.
MELIN, FRANK L.
MENDENHALL, MRS. MARY L.
MERRIAM, HENRY M.
MILLER, J. G.
*MILLER, L. S.
MITCHELL, JAY G.
MORGAN, F. N.
MORRISON, H. T.
MORRISON, MRS. H. T.
MOSELEY, W. H.
MUETH, JOHN, JR.
MUNSON, S. E.
MYERS, ALBERT
MYERS, JULIUS
MYERS, MRS. JULIUS
MYERS, LOUIS
    * Deceased

NEAL, JOHN R.
NELCH, B. F.
NELSON, OSCAR
NEWLIN, NORMA
NORBURY, FRANK P.
OSBORNE, GEORGIA L.
OWEN, M. G.
PADDOCK, J. H.
PALMER, GEORGE THOMAS
PARR, O. L.
PARSONS, A. J.
PASFIELD, GEORGE, JR.
PATTON, CHARLES L.
PATTON, WILLIAM L.
PAVEY, W. A.
PAYNE, EDWARD W.
PAYTON, JESSE K.
PHILLIPS, D. L.
PICKERING, JOHN L.
PICKERING, PAUL W.
PICCO, JOHN MARIA
PIERIK, HERMAN
POSTON, EMMETT
POTTER, FRED W.
PRATHER, R. V.
PRINCE, A. E.
PRINCE, MRS. A. E.
RANKIN, ALBERT H.
*RANKIN, HENRY B.
REES, THOMAS
REID, MRS. BURTON M.
REISCH, ALBERT
REISCH, GEORGE
RIEFLER, CHARLES J.
ROACH, CORWINE E.
ROBINSON, CHARLES H.
ROBINSON, MARGARET H.
ROBINSON, W. E.
RYAN, CHARLES DILLER
SALZENSTEIN, EMANUEL
SAMPSON, W. EDGAR
SAMUELS, LOUIS J.

SANKEY, JOHN E.
SCHAFF, M. D.
SCHLIPF, ALBERT C.
SCHLIPF, MRS. ALBERT C.
SCHMIDT, WILLIAM
SCHNEPP, JOHN S.
SCHUCK, CHARLES
SCOTT, MRS. EDGAR S.
SCOTT, O. G.
SELBY, MRS. PAUL
SHAND, RICHINGS J.
SHEPHERD, ALVA F.
SHUSTER, F. E.
SIKES, JOHN H.
SIMMONS, C. L.
SIMMONS, FRANK
SMITH, MRS. ANAIS C.
SMITH, BRAINERD H.
SMITH, DEWITT W.
SMITH, E. S.
SMITH, HAL M.
SMITH, WILLIAM W.
SNYDER, D. W.
SOLENBERGER, H. M.
SOLOMON, G. W.
SOLOMON, H. A.
SORLING, CARL A.
SOUTHER, LATHAM T.
SPAULDING, WILLIS J.
STALEY, E. E.
STEPHENS, R. ALLAN
STEPHENS, MRS. R. ALLAN

STERICKER, MRS. G. F.
STERN, EVA F.
STEVENS, A. D.
TAYLOR, WILL
THOMA, HENRY
THOMAS, JOHN T.
TOBIN, J. RALPH
TRIEBEL, A. J.
TROXELL, ROBERT W.
TRUTTER, FRANK L.
TUTTLE, H. H.
UHL, VICTOR A.
VOGEL, LESLIE H.
VREDENBURGH, REYNOLDS W.
VREDENBURGH, THOMAS II.
WALKER, JOHN H.
WALTERS, A. E.
WANLESS, CHARLES S.
WANLESS, FRED W.
WATTS, LAURA ELLA
WATTS, MRS. LAURA R.
WEAVER, G. E.
WEAVER, I. A.
WEAVER, MRS. I. A.
WHITE, MRS. CATHERINE DRESSER
WIEDLOCHER, FRANK
WIGGINS, LEWIS N.
WILCOXSON, R. J.
WILLIAMS, LUCY C.
WILLIAMSON, H. L.
WORKMAN, W. F.

NON-RESIDENT SUSTAINING MEMBERS

CALIFORNIA

BARKER, H. E.	*Los Angeles*
FREEMAN, E. M.	*Long Beach*
HOPPER, HARRY F.	*Pasadena*
KIMBER, THOMAS C.	*San Diego*
PASFIELD, A. H.	*La Jolla*

CALIFORNIA—(continued)

RISDON, F. RAY . . . . Los Angeles
RUSSELL, STUART . . . . Pasadena
SOLOMON, GEORGE E. . . . . Los Angeles
SOLOMON, R. C. JR. . . . . Los Angeles
WHEELER, W. W. . . . . Carmel-by-the-Sea

COLORADO

BARE, FRANK A. . . . . Denver

CONNECTICUT

FREEMAN, HARRISON B. . . . . Hartford
VROOM, MRS. CHARLOTTE T. . . . . Wallingford

DELAWARE

TALLMAN, FRANK G. . . . . Wilmington

ILLINOIS (Excluding Chicago)

ALEXANDER, E. D. . . . . Dixon
ARTHURS, W. C. . . . . Mt. Vernon
AUSTIN, H. W. . . . . Oak Park
BAXTER, E. A. . . . . Pawnee
BENNETT, W. W. . . . . Rockford
BLANE, F. E. . . . . Petersburg
BLUNK, S. M. . . . . Virden
*BONTJES, J. H. . . . . Peoria
BRITTIN, A. L. . . . . Athens
BROWN, MRS. MARY D. . . . . Lincoln
BROWN, B. W. . . . . Old Berlin
*BUNTAIN, C. M. CLAY. . . . . Kankakee
CAPPS, HARRY N. . . . . Jacksonville
CARLISLE, HENRY W. . . . . Evanston
CHURCH, WILLIAM T. . . . . Evanston
COLE, C. B. . . . . Chester
COOK, W. J. . . . . Winnetka
CUST, H. H. . . . . Mt. Vernon
DAVIS, DAVID . . . . Bloomington
DAWES, RUFUS C. . . . . Evanston
DODGE, DANIEL KILHAM . . . . Champaign
DUNCAN, C. M. . . . . Alton
DUNN, FRANK K. . . . . Charleston
FLING, JOHN W., JR. . . . . Wyoming
FUNK, DEANE M. . . . . McLean
GLANDON, ED. D. . . . . Pittsfield
* Deceased

GORDON, JAMES W. . . . . *Oquawka*
GOVERT, GEORGE W. . . . . *Quincy*
GROVES, WALTER G. . . . . *Carlinville*
HAND, FRED H. *Galva*
HAUBERG, JOHN . . . . *Rock Island*
HEARD, OSCAR E. . . . . *Freeport*
HIGBEE, HARRY . . . . *Pittsfield*
JACOB, EDWARD J. . . . . *Peoria*
JARMAN, LEWIS A. . . . . *Rushville*
JONES, NORMAN L. . . . . *Carrollton*
JONES, J. R. . . . . *Williamsville*
KEPLINGER, M. L. . . . . *Carlinville*
LAWRENCE, GEORGE A. . . . . *Galesburg*
LeFORGEE, C. C. . . . . *Decatur*
LILLARD, JOHN T. . . . . *Bloomington*
LILLARD, MRS. JOHN T. . . . . *Bloomington*
LITTLE, JOHN S. . . . . *Rushville*
LOWDEN, FRANK O. . . . . *Oregon*
LOWDEN, MRS. FRANK O. . . . . *Oregon*
McCLURE, J. E. . . . . *Carlinville*
MERRIAM, ALVIN O. . . . . *Auburn*
MILLER, FRANK T. . . . . *Peoria*
OAKLEAF, JOSEPH BENJAMIN. . . . . *Moline*
OGLESBY, JOHN G. . . . . *Elkhart*
ORENDORFF, U. G. . . . . *Canton*
PEASE, THEODORE C. . . . . *Urbana*
*PRATHER, J. F. . . . . *Williamsville*
PRATHER, MRS. J. F. . . . . *Williamsville*
PROVINE, WALTER M. . . . . *Taylorville*
RAMMELKAMP, CHARLES H. . . . . *Jacksonville*
RAYMOND, MRS. J. H. . . . . *Evanston*
REINBOLD, W. F. . . . . *Villa Park*
RENNICK, P. G. . . . . *Peoria*
RUBENS, JULES J. . . . . *Aurora*
RUSSELL, ANDREW . . . . *Jacksonville*
RYON, OSCAR B. . . . . *Streator*
SCHIRDING, HENRY . . . . *Petersburg*
SMITH, EUNICE C. . . . . *Alton*
SOLOMON, E. C. . . . . *Auburn*
STEVENSON, ADLAI E. . . . . *Bloomington*
STRAUS, MRS. JENNIE M. . . . . *Danville*
WAGNER, A. F. . . . . *Freeport*
   *Deceased

ILLINOIS (Excluding Chicago)—(continued)

WALLACE, Ross S. . . . . *Peoria*
WELDON, L. H. . . . . *Bloomington*
WILLIAMSON, THOMAS . . . . *Edwardsville*
WILLSON, H. T. *Virden*
WILSON, GEORGE H. . . . . *Quincy*

ILLINOIS—(Chicago)

ABBOTT, W. R.
ALLERTON, ROBERT
BALL, SIDNEY Y.
BABSON, GUSTAVUS
BABSON, HENRY
BARBEE, ROBERT E.
BARTHOLOMAY, HENRY
BLACK, JOHN D.
BOWEN, MRS. JOSEPH T.
BREWERTON, W. A.
BRIGGS, M. H.
BROWN, JAMES
BROWN, SCOTT
BUCKINGHAM, GEORGE T.
BUTLER, EDWARD B.
BUDD, BRITTON I.
BULLEN, CHARLES F.
BUTLER, RUSH C.
CARR, E. L.
CARRY, E. F.
CASSELS, EDWIN H.
CHAPMAN, THEODORE S.
CRANE, R. T., JR.
CUTTING, C. S.
DEAN, RICHMOND
DENEEN, CHARLES S.
DONNELLEY, THOMAS E.
DRAKE, TRACY
DUMMER, WILLIAM F.
DUMMER, MRS. WILLIAM F.
ECKHART, B. A.
EDENS, WILLIAM GRANT
ELSTON, I. C., JR.
FARWELL, ARTHUR L.

FARWELL, JOHN V.
FOREMAN, MILTON J.
FORGAN, DAVID R.
FOWLE, FRANK F.
GILCHRIST, JOHN F.
GLESSNER, JOHN J.
HAMBLETON, C. J.
HAMILL, CHARLES H.
*HAMILL, E. A.
HANNAH, A. W.
HARRISON, CARTER H.
HAY, H. COLLINS
HIRSHEIMER, L. D.
HORNER, HENRY
HULL, MORTON D.
HURD, H. B.
INSULL, SAMUEL
JONES, FRANK H.
JONES, W. CLYDE
JUDAH, NOBLE BRANDON
KING, WILLARD L.
KLINE, SOL
KNUDSON, S. O.
LAMON, JUDSON A.
LEE, JOHN H. S.
LEITER, JOSEPH
LOESCH, FRANK J.
MADLENER, ALBERT F.
MAGILL, HUGH S.
MARKHAM, C. H.
MARSHALL, THOMAS L.
MAYER, OSCAR F.
MAYER, OSCAR G.
McKINLOCK, GEORGE ALEXANDER

* Deceased

Meyer, Abraham
Meyer, Carl
Miller, Amos C.
Norman, Viola
Owsley, Mrs. Clara B.
Owsley, Heaton
Patten, Henry J.
Peabody, Stuyvesant
Peaks, George H.
Potts, Rufus M.
Prussing, Eugene E.
Ray, Verne
Reed, George W.
Reichman, Alexander F.
Rosenthal, James
Rosenthal, Lessing
Rosenwald, Julius
Russell, Edward
Sampsell, Marshall E.

Schaffner, Robert C.
Schmidt, Otto L.
Scott, John W.
Selz, J. Harry
Simpson, James
Snyder, Harry W.
Spencer, G. A.
Sprague, A. A.
Steinbrecher, Paul
Stern, A. W.
Stern, Alfred K.
Strawn, Silas H.
Thomas, Morris St P.
*Van Vechten, Ralph
Wacker, Charles H.
Wilcoxson, Arthur L.
Zane, John M.
Zimmerman, Herbert P.
   * Deceased

INDIANA

*Beveridge, Albert J. . . . . Indianapolis
Beveridge, Mrs. Albert J. . . . . Indianapolis
Carlisle, Mrs. C. A. . . . . South Bend
Coleman, C. B. . . . . Indianapolis
Fortune, William . . . . Indianapolis
Foster, Samuel K. . . . . Fort Wayne
Hall, Arthur F. . . . . Fort Wayne
Lewis, Charles S. . . . . Indianapolis
Lewis, Mrs. Mary P. . . . . Indianapolis
Rottger, C. H. . . . . Indianapolis
Warren, Louis A. . . . . Zionsville

IOWA

Bollinger, James W. . . . . Davenport
Cochrane, C. M. . . . . Davenport
Hamand, Jane . . . . Schaller
Jones, Henry Craig. . . . . Iowa City
Lindsay, Edwin B. . . . . Davenport
Lytle, H. J.. . . . . Davenport
Putnam, Elizabeth Duncan . . . . Davenport
Watts, W. A. . . . . Des Moines

KANSAS

Amos, J, J, ... *Humboldt*
Hall, Carrie A. . . . . *Leavenworth*

KENTUCKY

Townsend, W. H. . . . . *Lexington*
Mather, Otis M. . . . . *Hodgenville*

LOUISIANA

Hart, W. O. . . . . *New Orleans*

MARYLAND

Penniman, J. A. Dushane. . . . . *Baltimore*
Penniman, Mrs. J. A. Dushane. . . . . *Baltimore*
Stith, Mrs. Mary Johnson. . . . . *Baltimore*

MASSACHUSETTS

Barton, William E. . . . . *Foxboro*
Corneau, Mrs. Barton. . . . . *Boston*
Garfield, Irwin McDowell. . . . . *Boston*
Howell, Alfred Corey. . . . . *Dedham*
Lord, Robert H. . . . . *Boston*
Loring, Mrs. Robert G. . . . . *Lexington*
Tracy, W. W. . . . . *Williamstown*

MICHIGAN

Henkle, Thomas H. . . . . *Detroit*
Mackie, Donald Montgomery. . . . . *Jackson*
Minary, C. K. . . . . *Benton Harbor*
Simons, W. H. . . . . *Coldwater*
Schilling, George A. . . . . *Detroit*
Tippy, C. W. . . . . *Jackson*

MINNESOTA

Arnold, O. J. . . . . *Minneapolis*

MISSISSIPPI

Sage, H. K. . . . . *Clarksdale*

MISSOURI

Cotter, S. E. . . . . *St. Loius*
Gambrill, George C. . . . . *St. Louis*
Jones, James C. . . . . *St. Louis*
Marney, John D.. . . . . *St. Louis*

NEW HAMPSHIRE

WINANT, JOHN G. . . . . *Concord*

NEW JERSEY

DUFFIELD, EDWARD D. . . . . *Newark*
HELLER, R. ARTHUR. . . . . *Newark*
RICHARDSON, W. H. . . . . *Jersey City*
STERN, J. DAVID . . . . *Camden*
TOMLINSON, R. E. . . . . *Montclair*
WARD, WM. R. *Newark*

NEW YORK

ARMSBY, GEORGE N. . . . . *New York*
BARNES, HENRY B. . . . . *New York*
BARTHOLD, W. H. . . . . *New York*
BECHTEL, E. J. . . . . *New York*
CADWELL, E. B. . . . . *New York*
COBB, B. C. . . . . *New York*
DURYEE, P. S. . . . . *New York*
FRAKER, GEORGE W. . . . . *New York*
GREENMAN, FREDERICK F. . . . . *New York*
HARDY, GEORGE E. . . . . *New York*
HERTZ, EMANUEL. . . . . *New York*
HUTTON, MRS. E. F. . . . . *New York*
JACKSON, STUART W. . . . . *New York*
JELLEY, SUSAN BYFORD . . . . *New York*
KENNEY, T. A. . . . . *New York*
KIRBY, H. N. . . . . *New York*
LEHMAN, J. HOWARD . . . . *New York*
LIEB, J. W. . . . . *New York*
LISMAN, F. J. . . . . *New York*
MAGILL, ROSWELL F. . . . . *New York*
MESERVE, FREDERICK H. . . . . *New York*
MITCHELL, CHARLES E. . . . . *New York*
MORROW, MRS. HONORE WILLSIE. . . . . *New York*
OCHS, ADOLPH . . . . *New York*
OTHEMAN, ROSWELL C. . . . . *New York*
PATTERSON, J. M. . . . . *New York*
PRICE, JACOB L. . . . . *New York*
PUPIN, MICHAEL . . . . *New York*
REED, MRS. GEORGIANA CONKLING. . . . . *Larchmont*
REED, WALDO S. . . . . *New York*
ROBERTS, NICHOLAS . . . . *New York*

NEW YORK—(continued)

SCHWEDTMAN, F. C. . . . . *New York*
*SHEDD, J. A. . . . . *New York*
SHEPPARD, JOHN S. . . . . *New York*
SMYTHE, BENJAMIN E. . . . . *Brooklyn*
STRONG, CHARLES H. . . . . *New York*
THORNE, SAMUEL . . . . *New York*
VANDERLIP, F. A. . . . . *Scarborough*
WEADOCK, JOHN C. . . . . *New York*
WEIL, FRANK L. . . . . *New York*
WHITE, CHARLES T. . . . . *Brooklyn*
*WHITNEY, PAYNE . . . . *New York*
WHITNEY, MRS. PAYNE . . . . *New York*

OHIO

BLINN, A. C. . . . . *Akron*
CORSON, O. T. . . . . *Oxford*
HOLDEN, GUERDON S. . . . . *Cleveland*
HOLDEN, MRS. GUERDON S. . . . . *Cleveland*

OREGON

MAGILL, SEWARD LINCOLN . . . . *Lostine*

PENNSYLYVANIA

BROWN, JAMES CROSBY. . . . . *Philadelphia*
WIGGINS, HORACE LELAND. . . . . *Philadelphia*

TENNESSEE

JOHNSON, W. W. . . . . *Memphis*

UTAH

HOWARD, EDWARD C. . . . . *Salt Lake City*

VERMONT

WILLIAMS, NORMAN . . . . *Woodstock*

WASHINGTON

BISSETT, CLARK PRESCOTT. . . . . *Seattle*

WEST VIRGINIA

GOODYKOONTZ, WELLS . . . . *Williamson*
    *Deceased

WISCONSIN

*ENOS, GEORGE T. . . . . *Waukesha*
FRENCH, HARRY L. . . . . *Madison*
HAMBRECHT, GEORGE P. . . . . *Madison*
NEFF, G. C. *Madison*
STONE, NAT . . . . *Milwaukee*

DISTRICT OF COLUMBIA

CORNWALL, LUTHER M. . . . . *Washington*
DAWES, CHARLES G. . . . . *Washington*
HATCH, FRANK L. . . . . *Washington*
NICOLAY, HELEN . . . . *Washington*
PALMER, JOHN MCAULEY . . . . *Washington*
PAYNE, JOHN BARTON. . . . . *Washington*
WADSWORTH, MRS. J. H. JR. . . . . *Washington*

BELGIUM

WHITLOCK, BRAND. . . . . *Brussels*

FRANCE

JAY, N. D. . . . . *Paris*

CONTRIBUTORS TO ENDOWMENT

MR. AND MRS. IRA B. BLACKSTOCK
JANE LOGAN BROWN
OWSLEY BROWN
*MRS. STUART BROWN
ALICE EDWARDS BUNN
*JACOB BUNN
MRS. JACOB BUNN
HENRY BUNN, II.
JACOB BUNN, II.
MILDRED BUNN, II.
GEORGE W. BUNN
ALBERT E. CONVERSE
HENRY A. CONVERSE

CHARLES G. DAWES
CHARLES S. DENEEN
MRS. LUCY W. DICKERMAN
JOHN H. FINLEY
MR. AND MRS. FRANK L. HATCH
MR. AND MRS. OZIAS M. HATCH
OZIAS M. HATCH, JR.
MR. AND MRS. PASCAL ENOS HATCH
LOGAN HAY
MRS. LOGAN HAY
MARY DOUGLAS HAY
J. H. HOLBROOK
MRS. GUERDON HOLDEN

* Deceased

MARY, MAUDE, RUTH AND GRACE
  HUMPHREY
FRANCIS P. IDE
MRS. FRANCIS P. IDE
ROBERT C. LANPHIER
HENRY M. MERRIAM
JULIUS M. MYERS
HELEN NICOLAY
MRS. CLARA B. OWSLEY

JOHN MCAULEY PALMER
GEORGE PASFIELD, JR.
MICHAEL PUPIN
CHARLES SCHUCK
DEWITT WICKLIFF SMITH
ROBERT ALLAN STEPHENS
*PHILIP BARTON WARREN
MRS. PHILIP BARTON WARREN
   *Deceased